Thank you to Pilar, Michele, and the Lorax

PERCEVAL PRESS

Coincidence of Memory: Viggo Mortensen

Vol. 1, no. 1
ISBN 1-889195-49-9

Sixth Edition

Published by Perceval Press
www.percevalpress.com

Editor: Pilar Perez
Design: Michele Perez
Copy Editor: Sherri Schottlaender
Digital Mastering: Hugh Milstein

Printed in Spain at Jomagar, S/A

Cover image: *Sueño del Retiro*, 2001

COINCIDENCE OF MEMORY

VIGGO MORTENSEN

PERCEVAL

Lullaby

Can't hear.
Keep listening
to the right song
come up in a
drop
that runs
across the wall
and hangs
on the doorknob.
Sing together
across the city
squeeze a note
that stays in your fist
pulling your hair.

(1992)

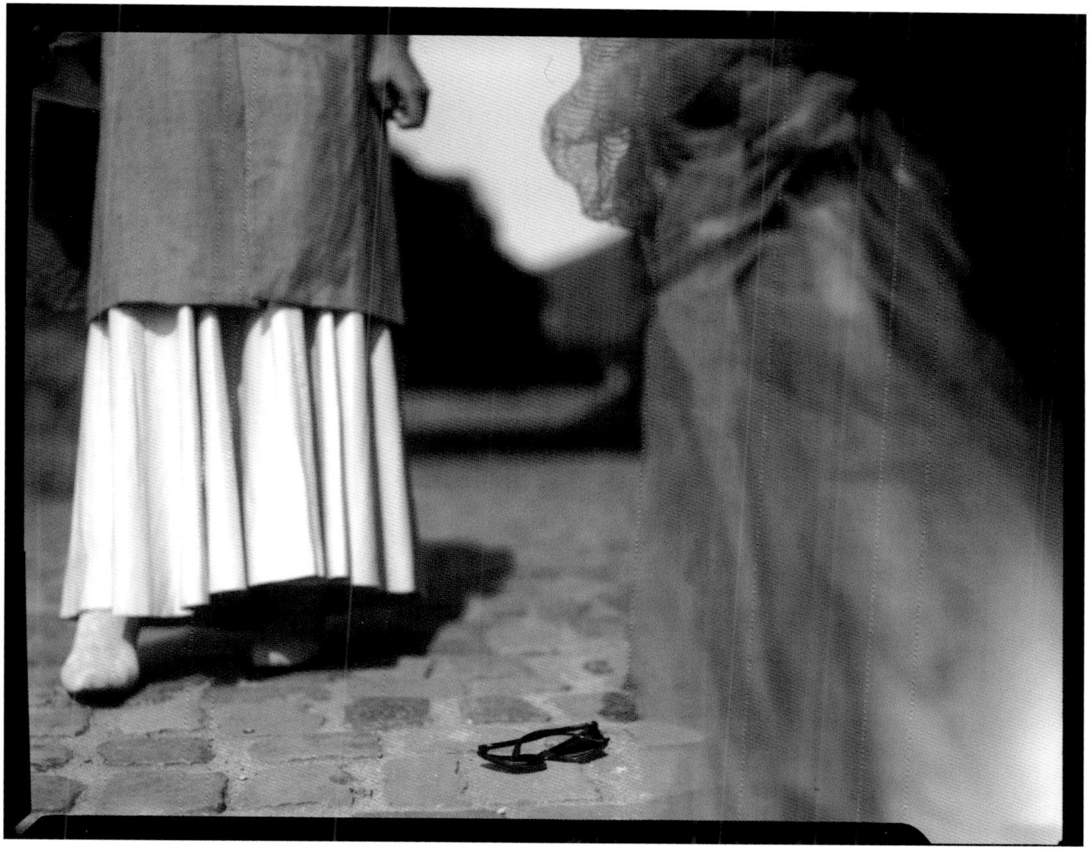

The Low Countries, 2001

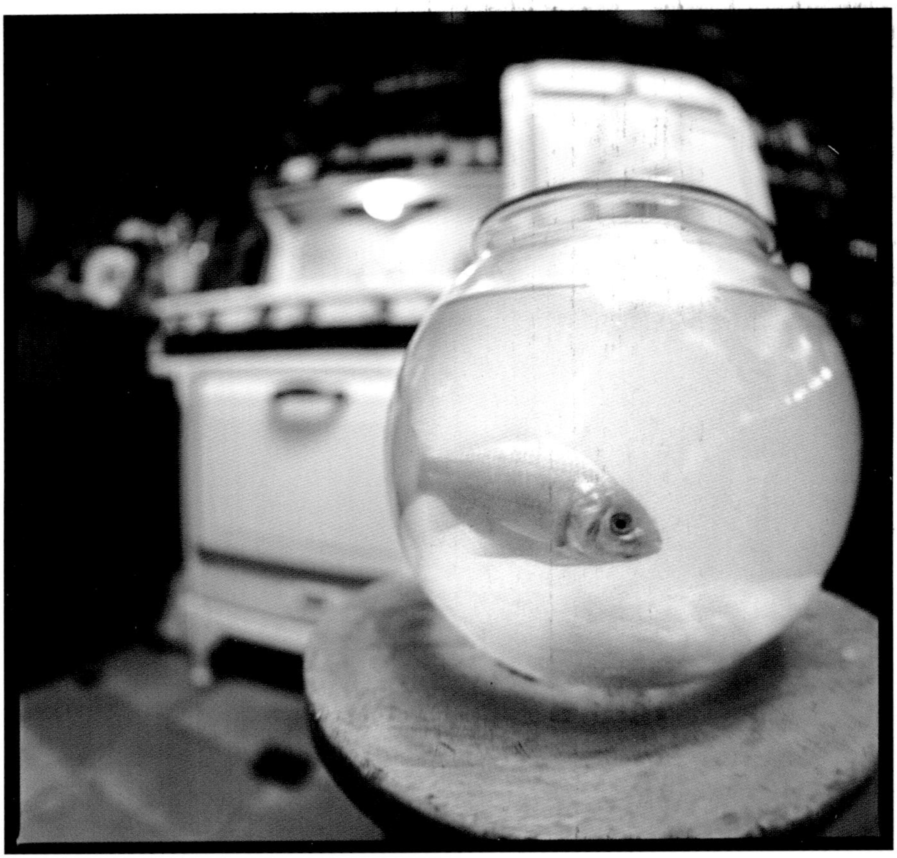

Friday, 1996

Clear

I first heard your voice from an airplane. You told me you had crystal knees and couldn't stop thinking about Jean Seberg's foetus baby in its glass coffin to prove it wasn't black at all. I wanted to hang up or politely say goodbye and then change my number and never answer the phone again until I knew you were dead. But you kept saying things I wanted to hear, like that a window might as well be a wall but thank God for fish tanks and bottles.

(1995)

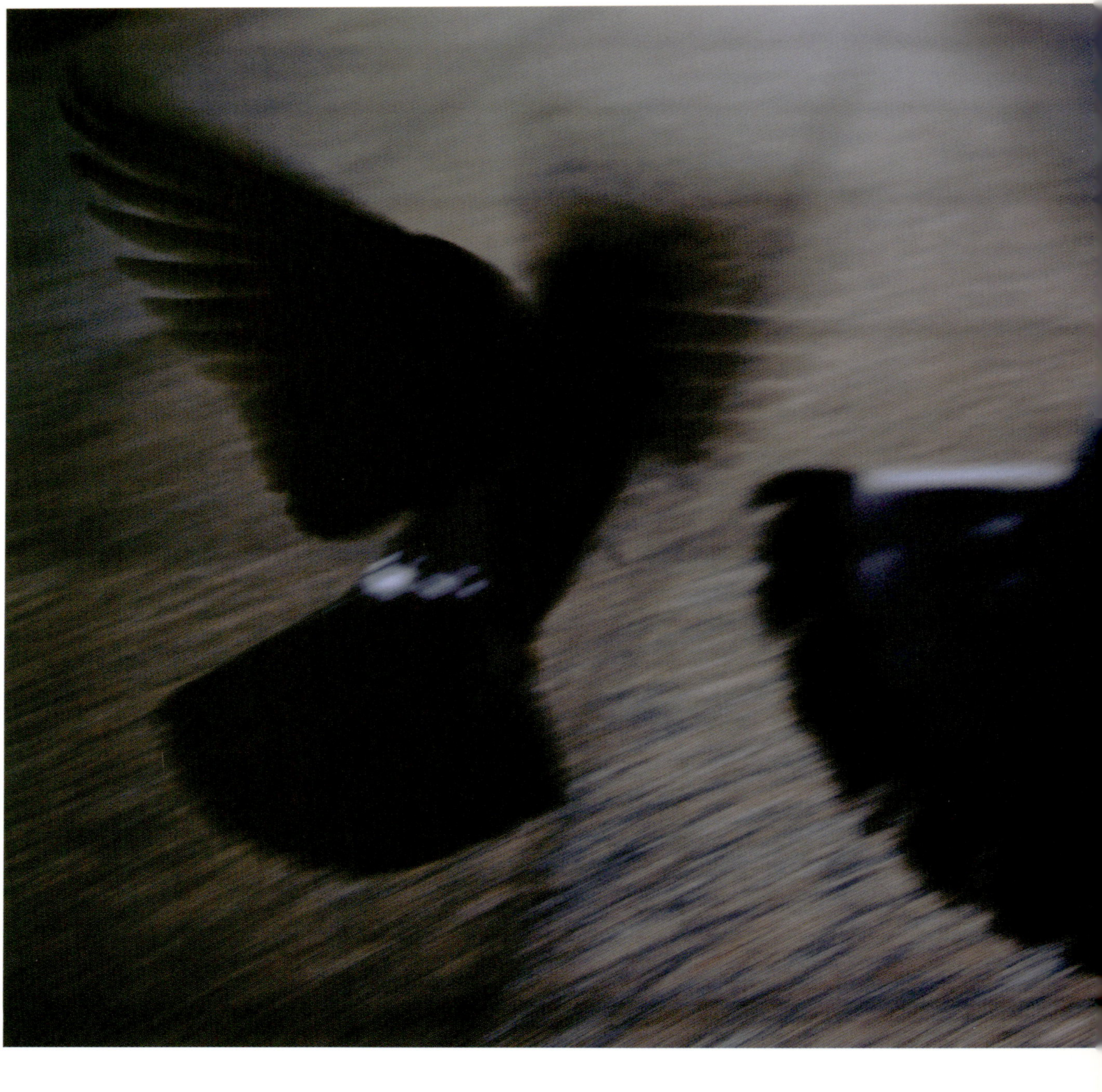

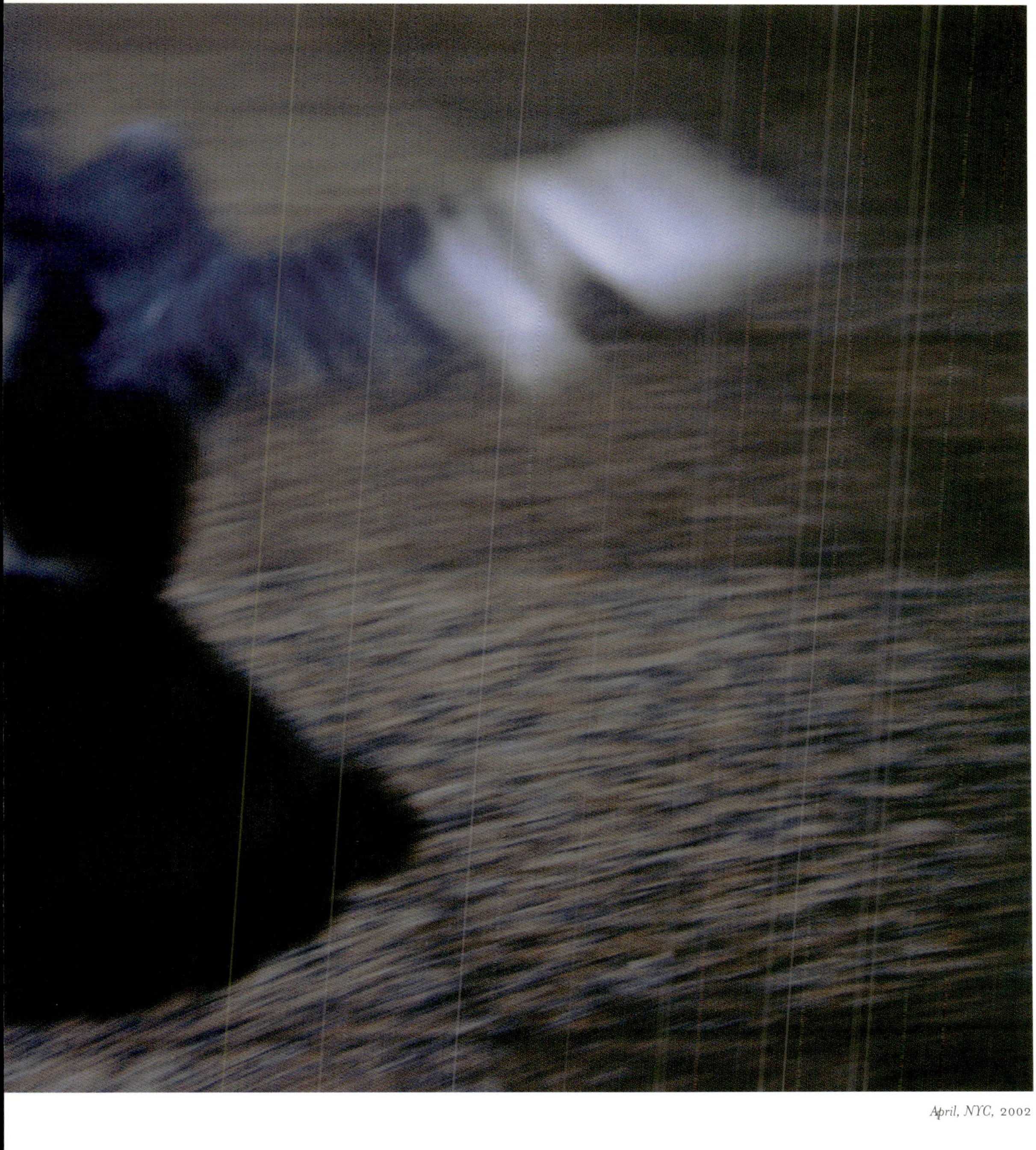

April, NYC, 2002

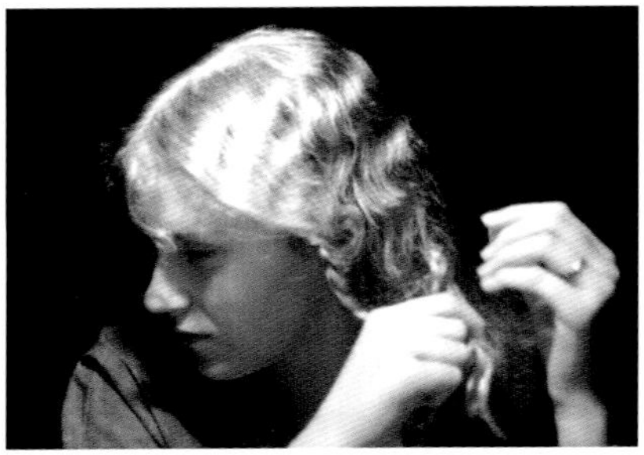

Ruth, 1978

Wooed her like a dolphin,
treats her like tuna.
She blackens, tries experiencing
nothing. He looks for her
without touching, makes pinpricks
in her furtive nakedness,
like a hyena.

Flooded plains may remind her
of startled fish, sunken palaces
lit by moons and moons.
He does not know what she's
thinking, doesn't know what's worse:
believing she's come straight
from heaven or nowhere
at all.

She is willing to continue
feeding him himself; calls that
living on her own terms,
safe in houses they promise
to build each other with
views on every side and
enough curtain to sleep
through it all.

(1996)

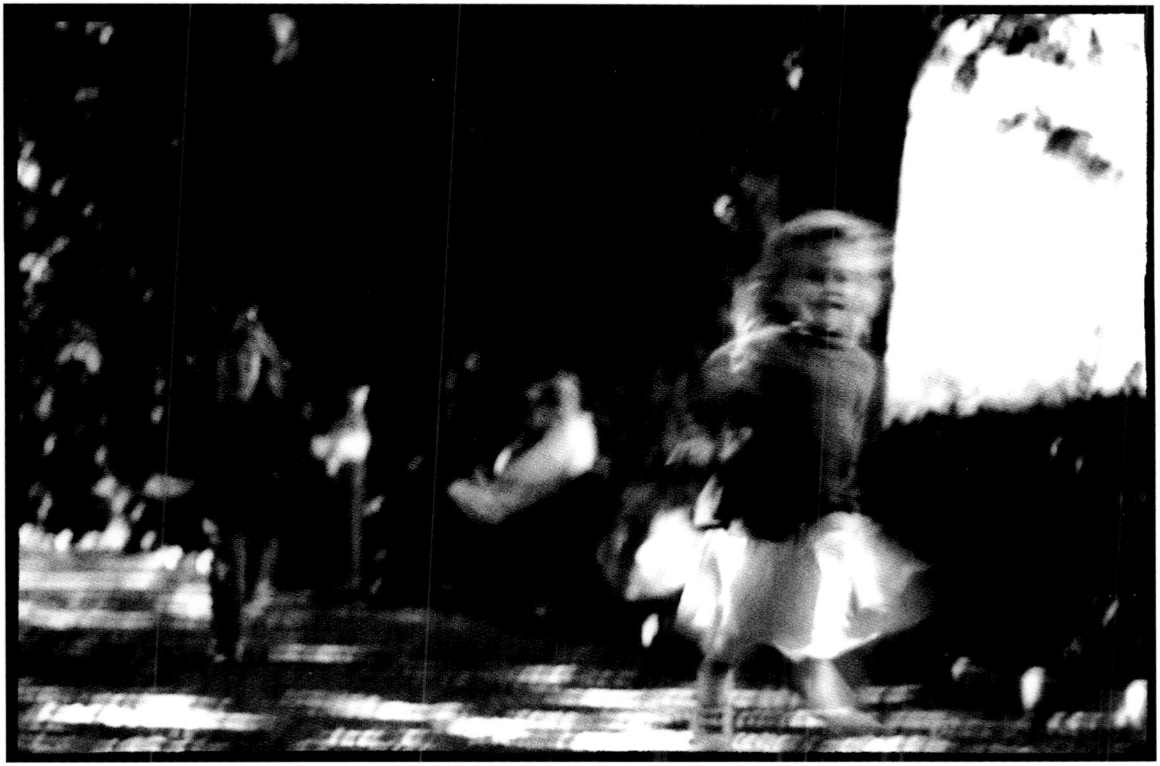

Roma, October, 1995

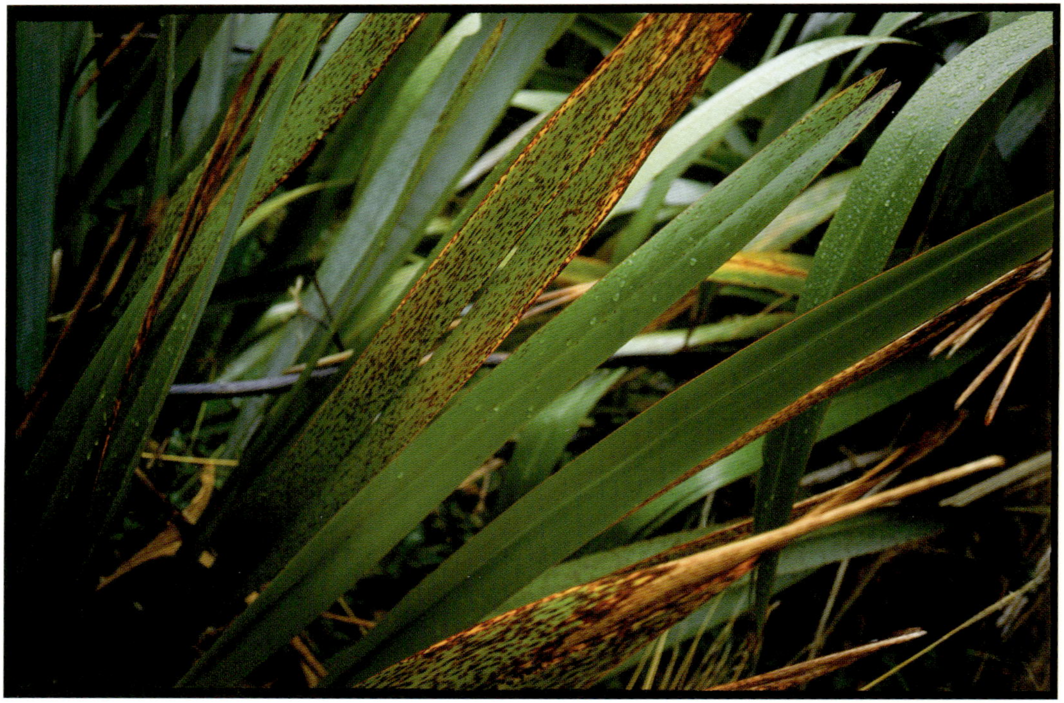

Green #12, 2000

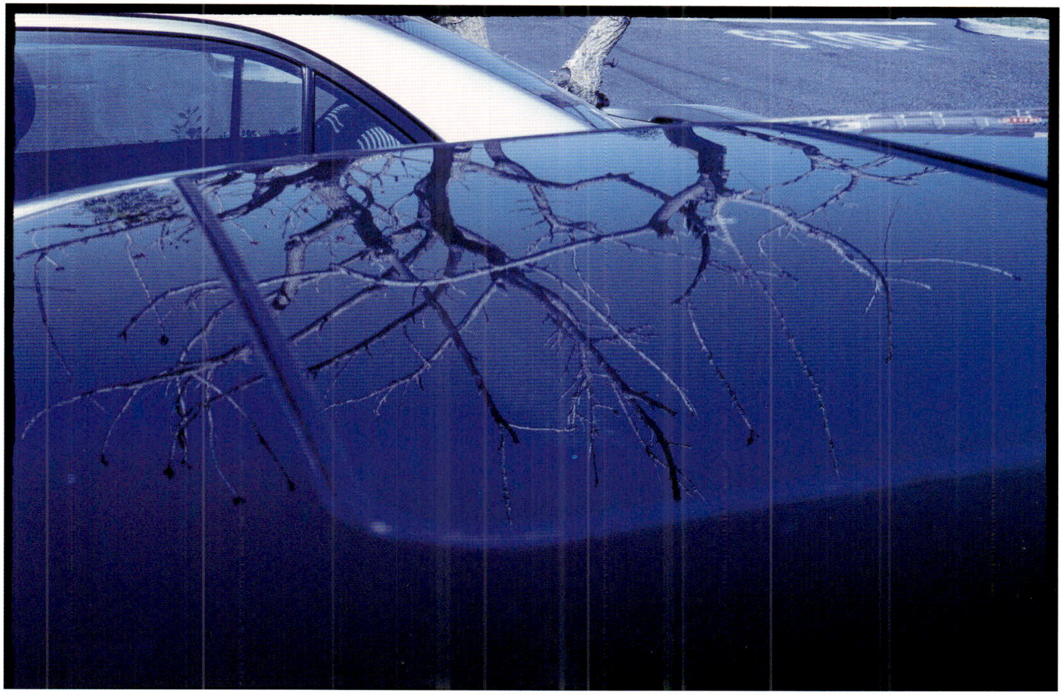

Ventura #2, 2002

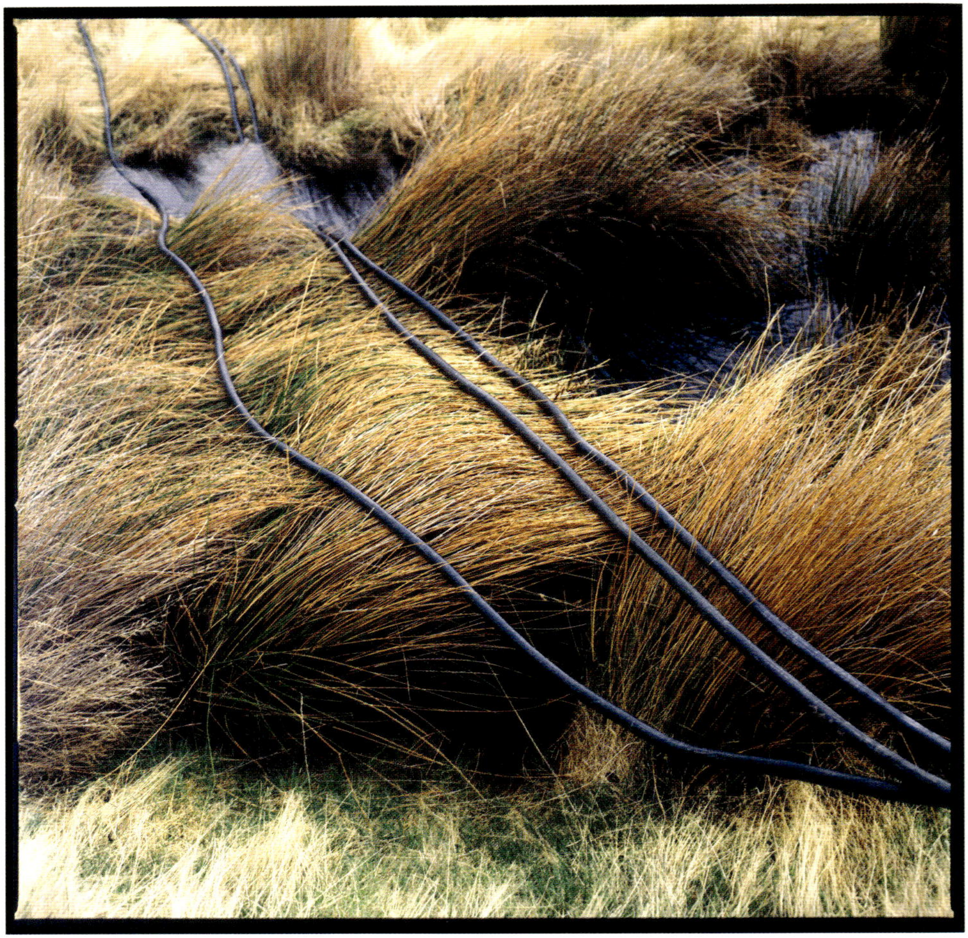

Intrusion #8, 2000

Weekends

Medicated limbs, lonely and greedy. Sick for attention, dying for company, you're drunk for days. Overburdened, moss-rotten branches heave slowly with the weak night breeze, like a failing heart, and graze the stone wall.

The nurse in me won't let me leave.

Homemade illness hardens into sugar and batters your speech, draping your dry white tongue over your teeth. Red pinholes for eyes, and your mouth is a smudge.

Do I have to watch tomorrow afternoon while you keep your face warm with the television and the maple drips on the lawn chairs that flake and rust on the flooded terrace?

When you start snoring, I'll take the tray from your lap and tip you over so I can look for the rest of your lunch under the green sofa cushions and probably find those pills you've been hiding. By the time the clouds dim and I start seeing us in the windows, I'll be drunk myself and ready to wake you for dinner.

(1985)

Five Thousand Years

It's a long, long way
made of stone
from Omaha to Cairo.
From the riverbank
through the dying fields
across the sea
to the bloody quarries
where they keep digging
for rulers
while school bells
echo
north and south
off the twin brown
mirrors of the Missouri
and the Nile.

(1991-92)

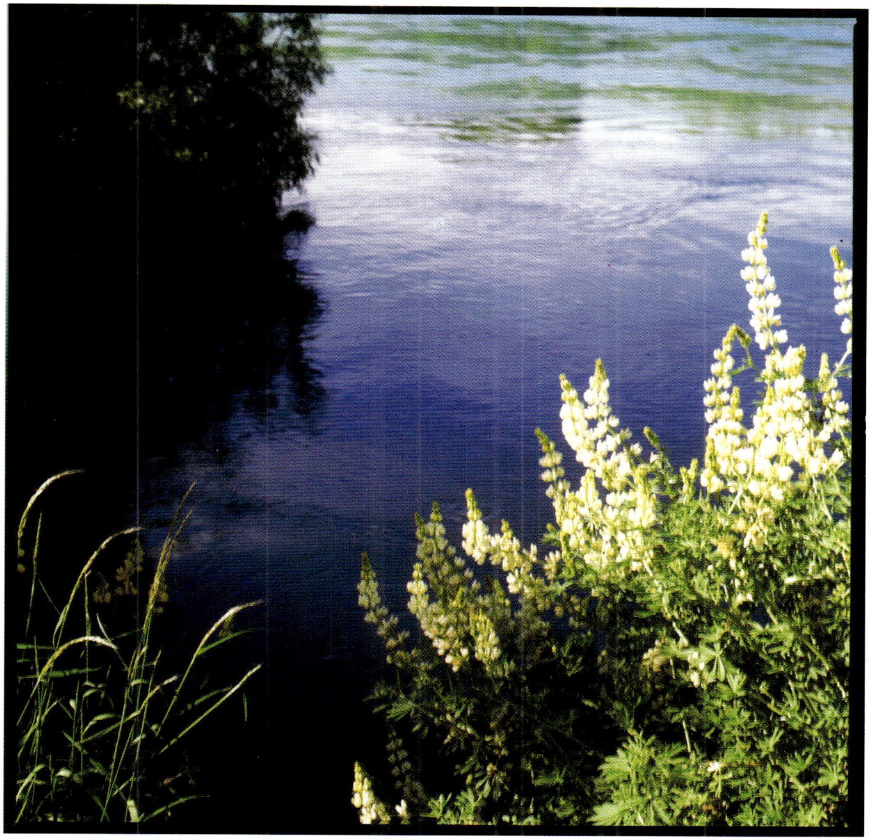

Kawarau #2, 1999

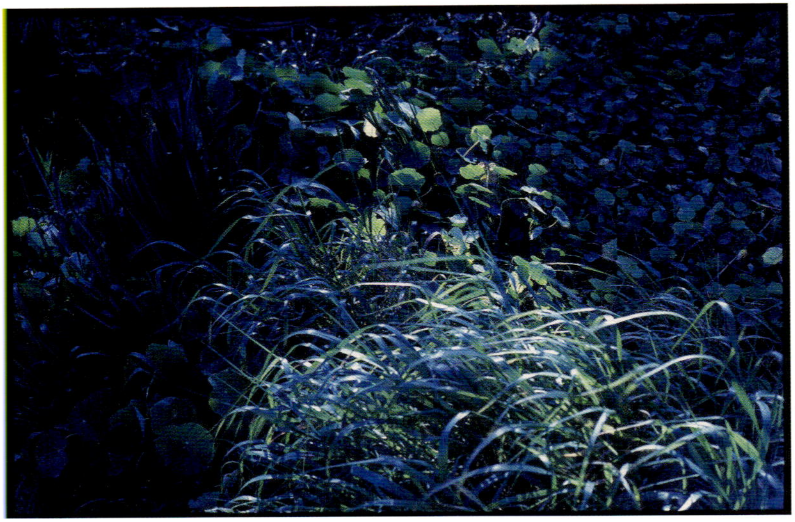

Ventura, 2002

Chaco

Me cago en la selva
como los monos
con sus dientes
perfectos y amarillos
sin tenerle miedo
a ningun tigre.

(1995)

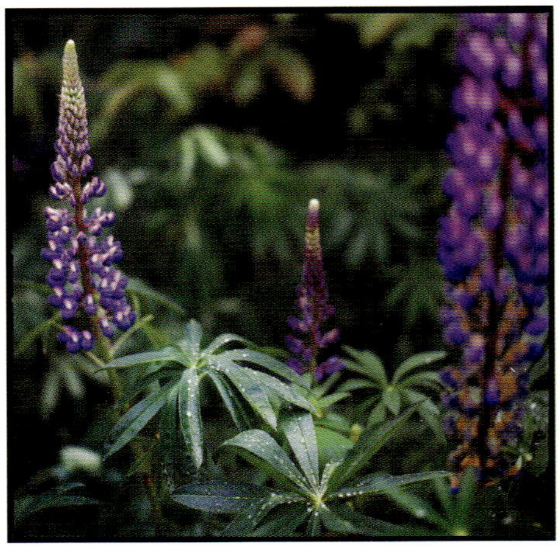

Wakatipu, 1999

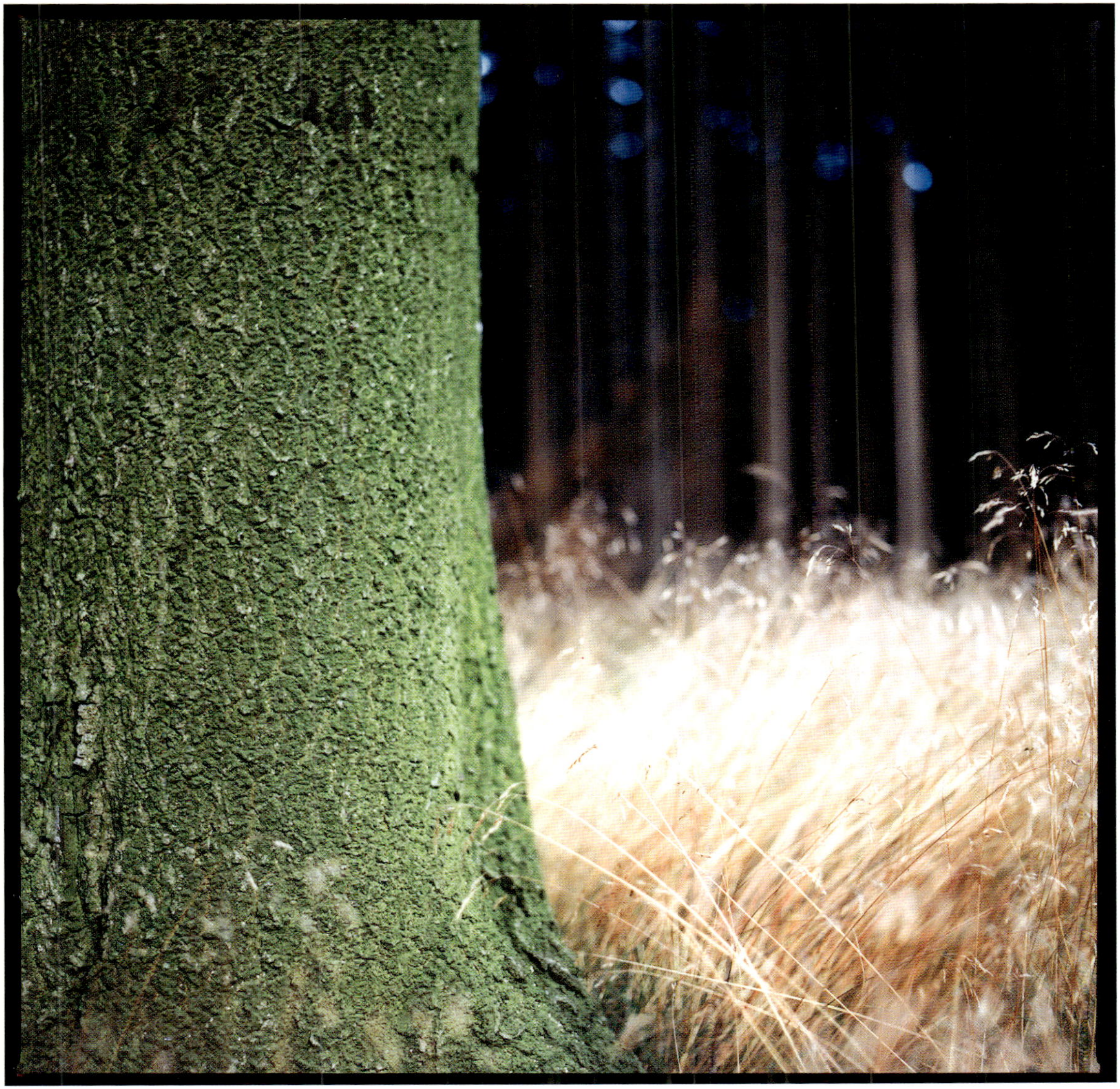

Saxon, 1994

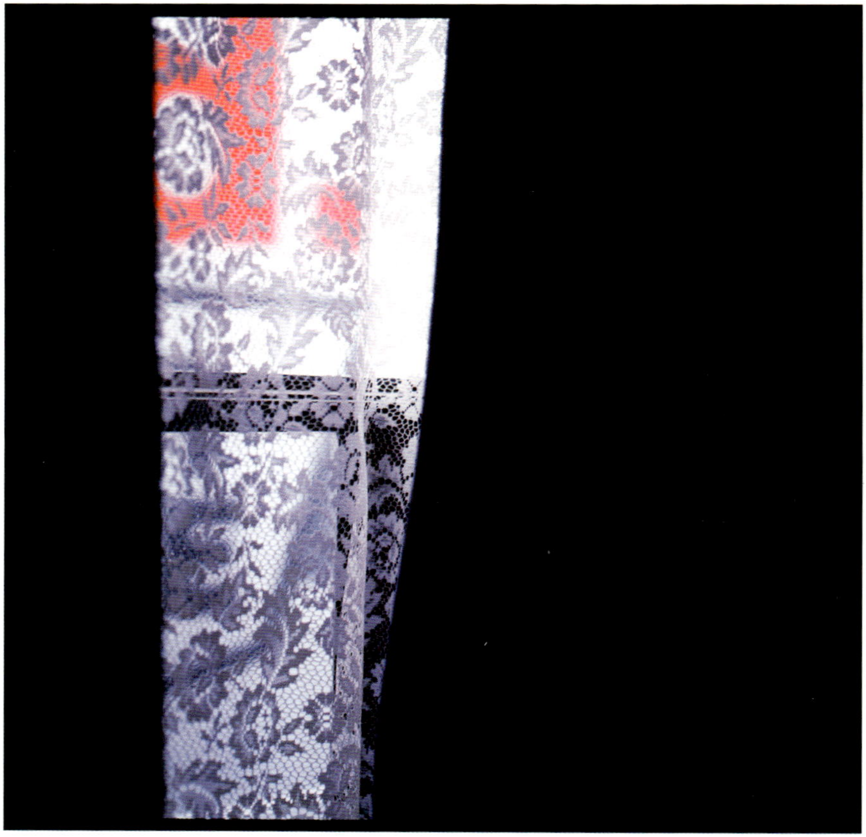

d., 2000

Hillside

We underestimate damage
done to the sky
when we allow words
to slip away
into the clouds.

I remember making promises
to you outside. We
were watching flowers
that hadn't opened.
A bee darted, careful
not to stick to
your half-shut mouth.

(1994)

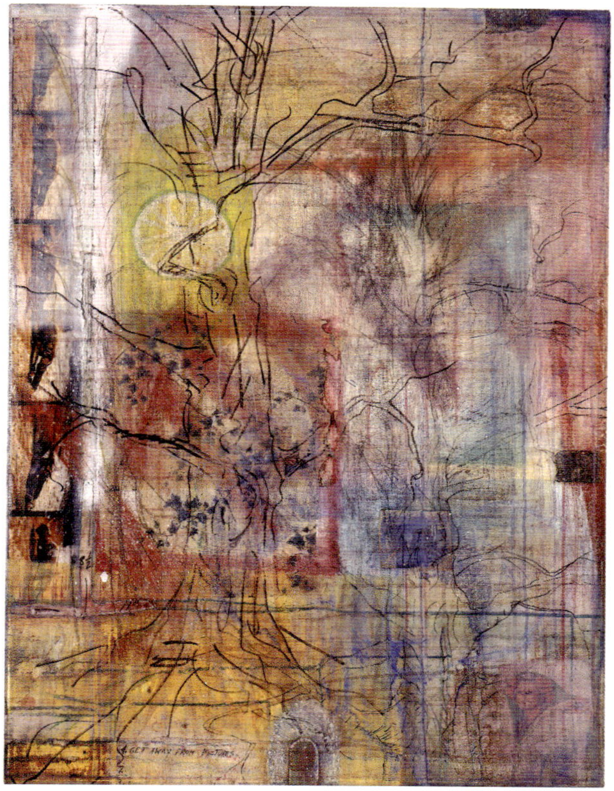

After Darkly Noon, 1999–2002

Apart

You found my keys
on an angel's hip
moved half the fallen trees
from the frozen road.

This trip is
all I thought
it would be
and we're not
even ½ way yet.

If I can't touch you
with snow-hung firs
our only witnesses
can't have your eyes
when everyone's asleep
then the fire's almost out.

You ask the un-named
attraction to leave town
but keep checking
if I'm still around.

Should we sidestep
putting fingers to
words tracing lips that
would inform us?

Once said I'd missed
you every instant
before we'd met.
Now believe we knew
how sad we'd be
apart.

(1999–2000)

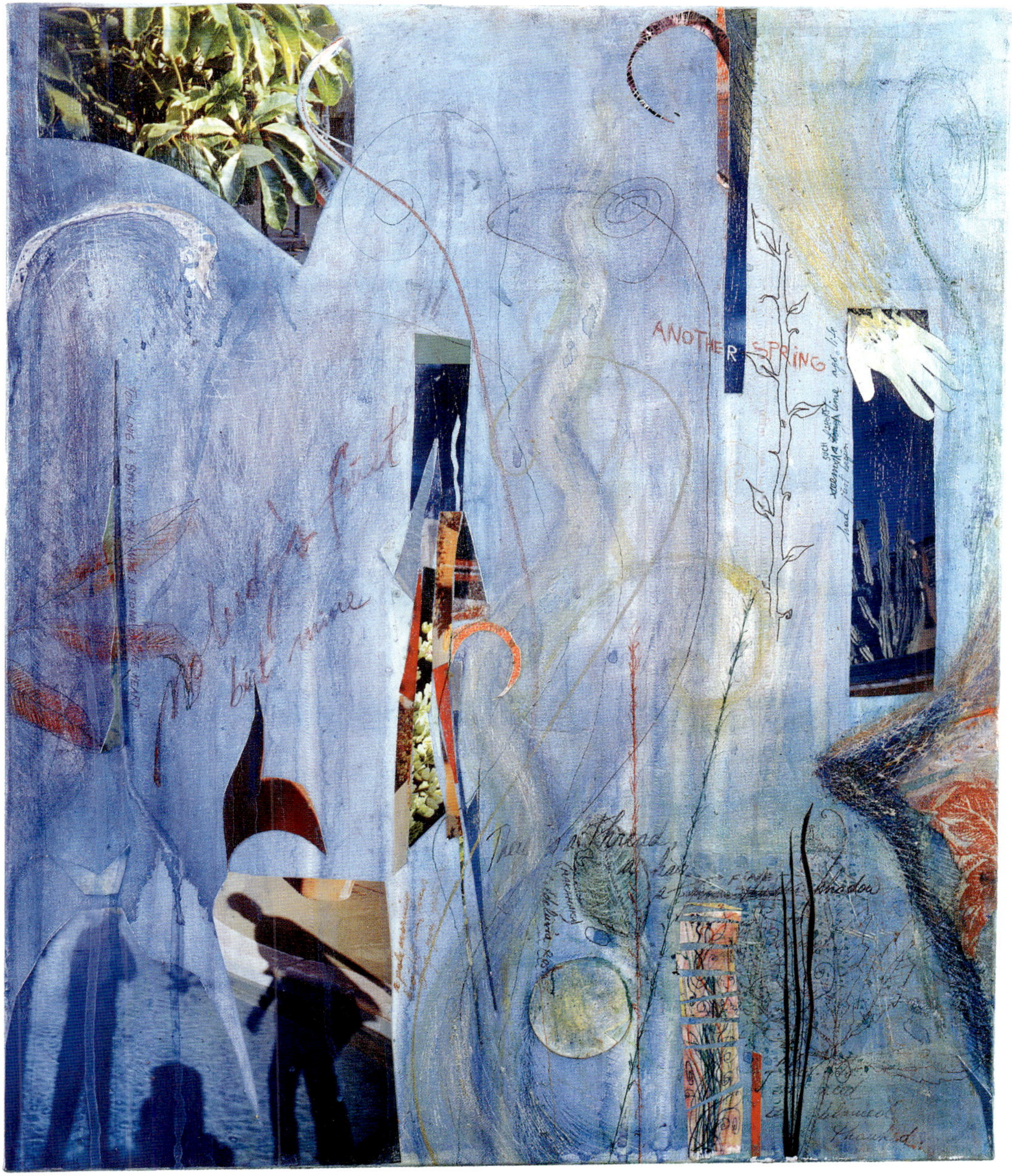

Another Spring, 2000

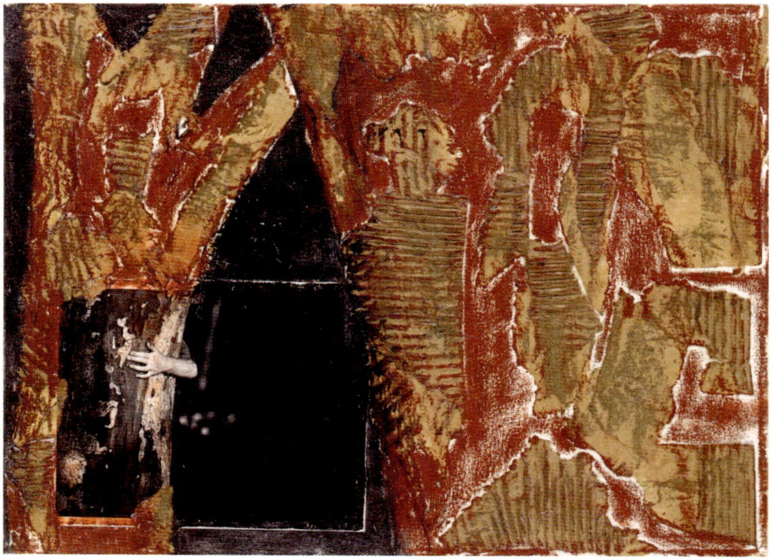

Indiana, 1997–98

Matinee

After years of merging
and allowing yourself
to be assimilated
your hair and clothes
have turned brown.
Then one afternoon
you leave a theatre
after taking in the
restored version of
"The Hero Returns" and
find yourself wanting to
be treated special.

(1997)

Keepsake

Still unused
the letter opener
she got on her birthday
has become tarnished.
It lies on the sill
next to a seashell
she found in Florida
before moving west.
Before becoming a writer.
Before becoming a mother.
Her son wants to use it
as a dagger, to
wield it savagely
against monsters
streaming from toy-
cluttered corners
of his room
but he can't
reach it yet.

(1991)

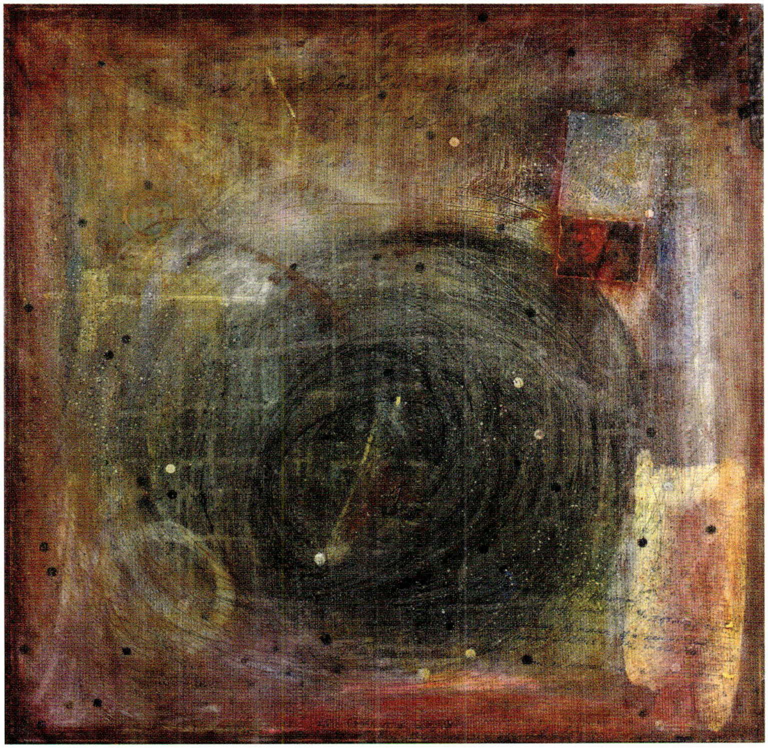

Kissinger Dream, 1999–2002

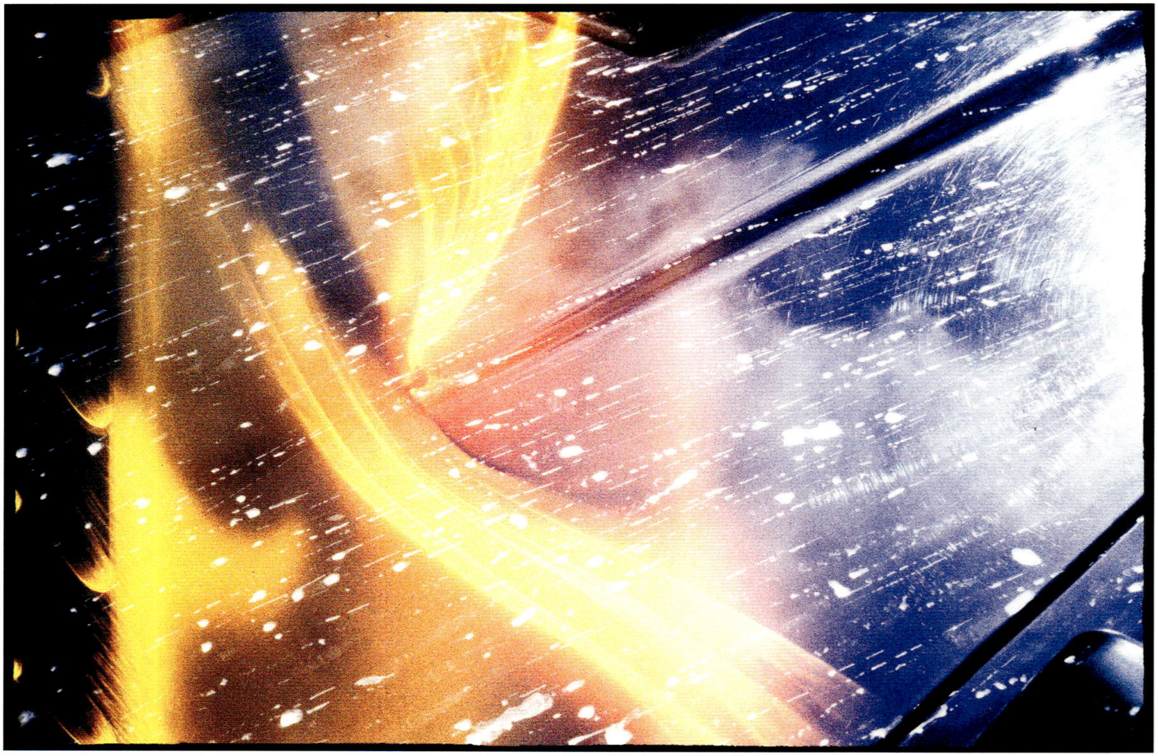

Noon, 2000

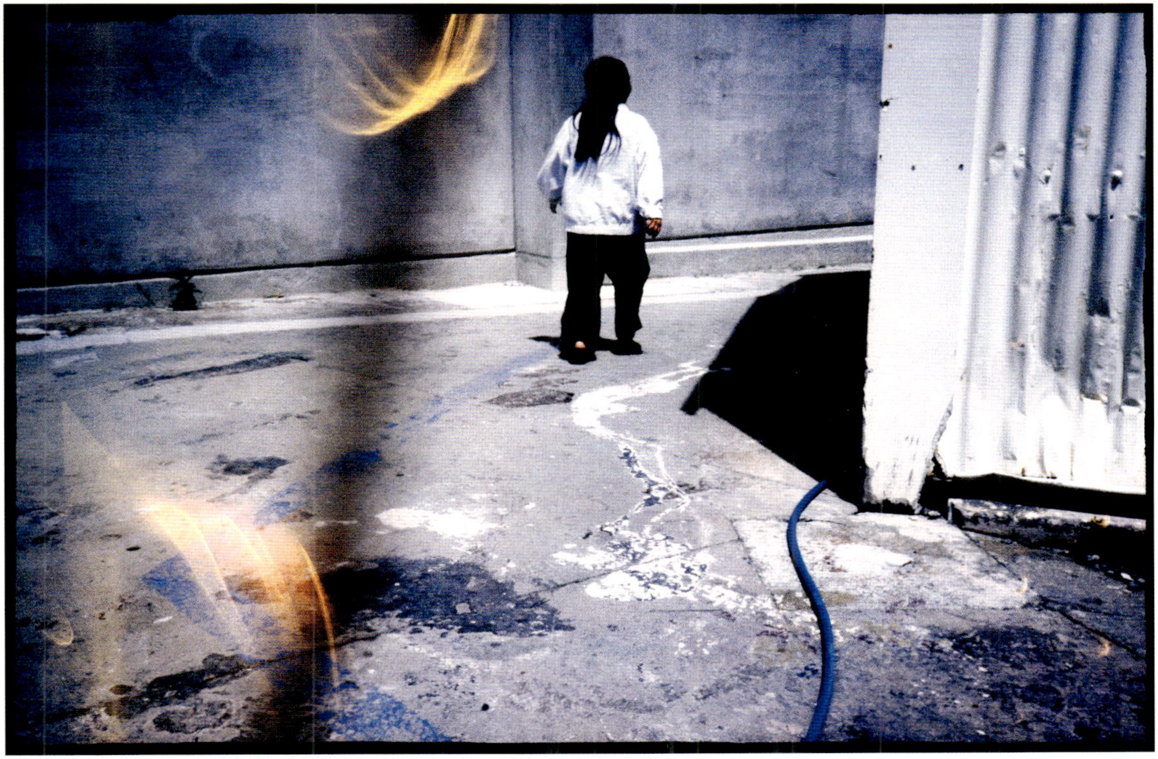

Fon, 2000

Fossils

1.
Red-eyed, chore laden
and stooped with grudges
they scratch on the sheepridges
with their bleached sticks
knuckles flaring in the cold
and pick a living from the sand.

There are no seducers
no bowls of fruit carved from teak.
Shards of bone china
are occasionally exposed
in the eroding cliffs
stubborn testaments
to hopeful Sunday evenings
frozen faithful and waiting
for spring.
The only thing green
is the now scurrying
now stone-still lizard
son of the permanent footprints
that mark fitful starts
to invisibled paths
in the bankrupt riverbed.

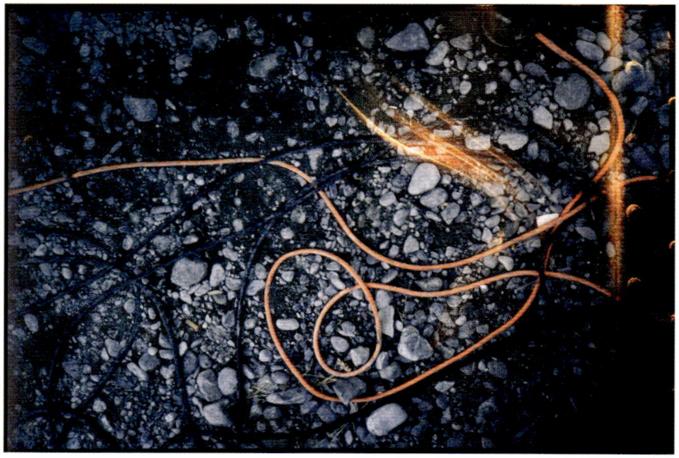

Delay, 2000

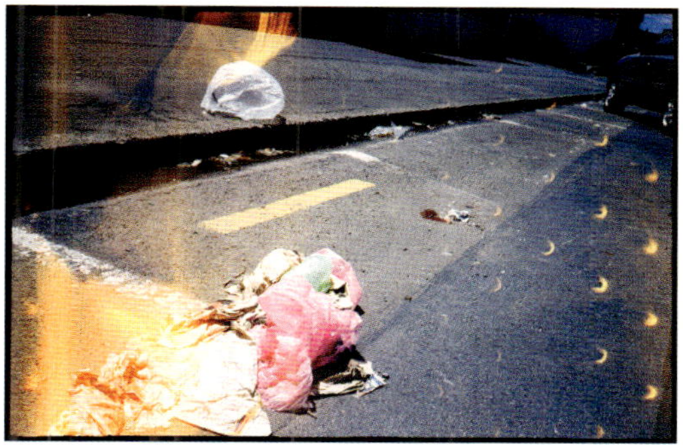

Shipshape #6, 2000

2.

THE WOMEN CRAWL
WITH UNVARYING PULSES
BEARING RUSTING PAILS
OF DISCARDED SHALE
FOR SLEEPWALKING HUSBANDS
WITH HANDS THAT DREAM
OF SKINNING FISH
AFTER TEARING ENTRAILS
FROM SUPPLE YOUNG SPINES.

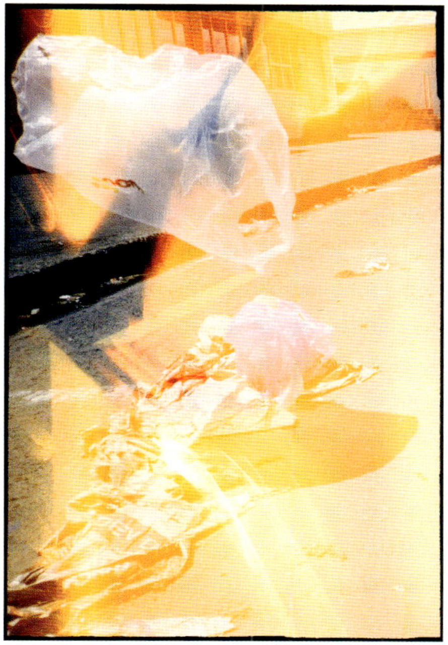

Shipshape #3, 2000

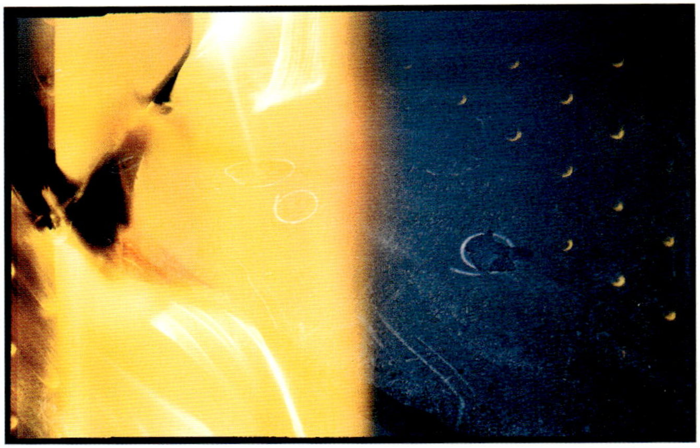

Shipshape #2, 2000

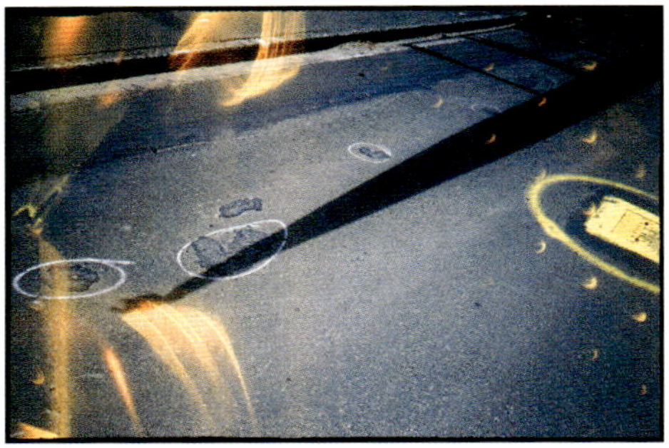

Shipshape, 2000

3.

There are no children
only younger versions
of those nearly done.
Good likenesses
of the same lack
of a warm side
of the same limited repertoire
of mannerisms
of the same inflexibility
of lifespans.

The grey birds call thinly
from thirsty sandstone perches
as the light finally weakens
and somewhere
up in the charred pines
you can hear
the beginning of the wind.

(1992)

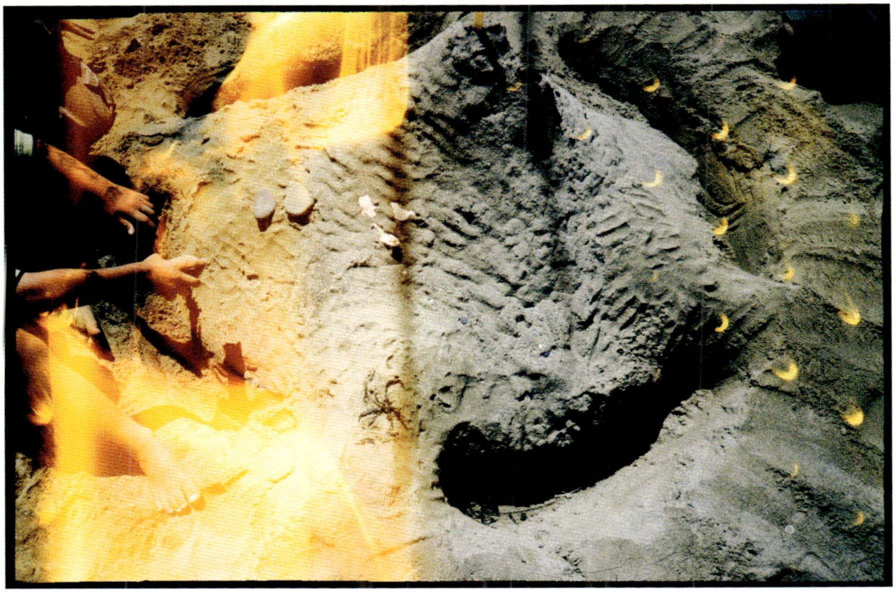

Shipshape #5, 2000

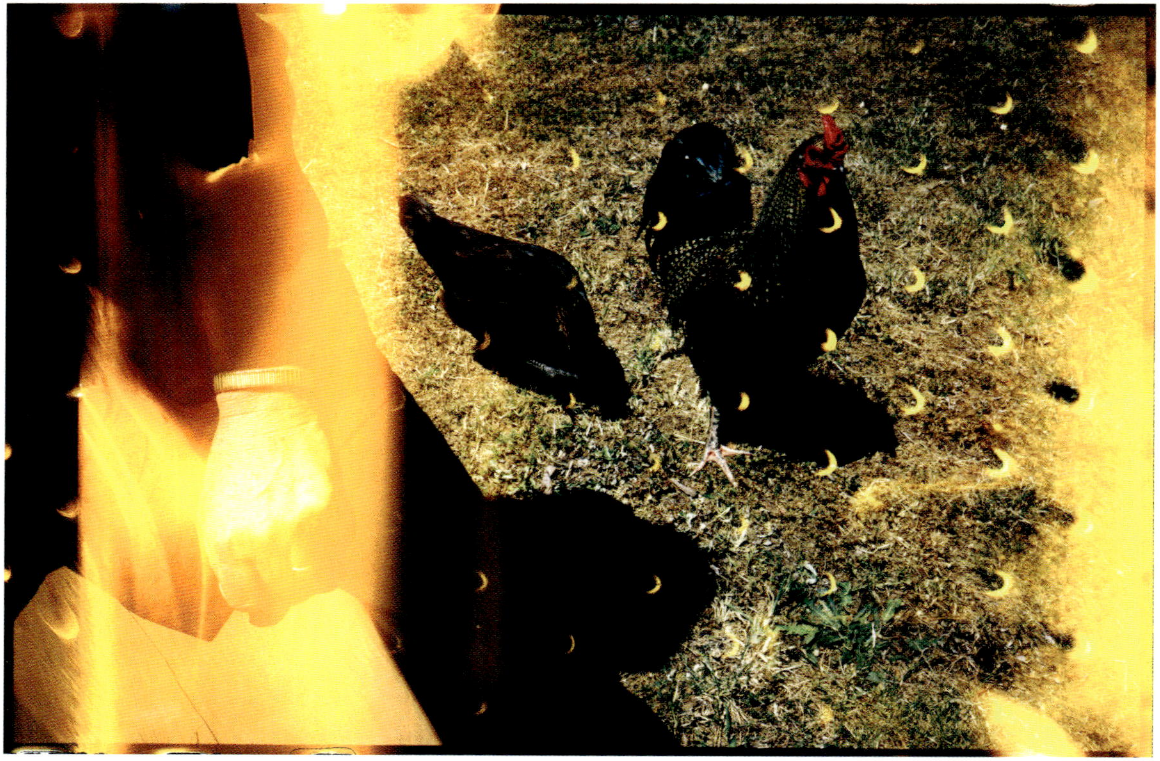

There's That Cock, 2000

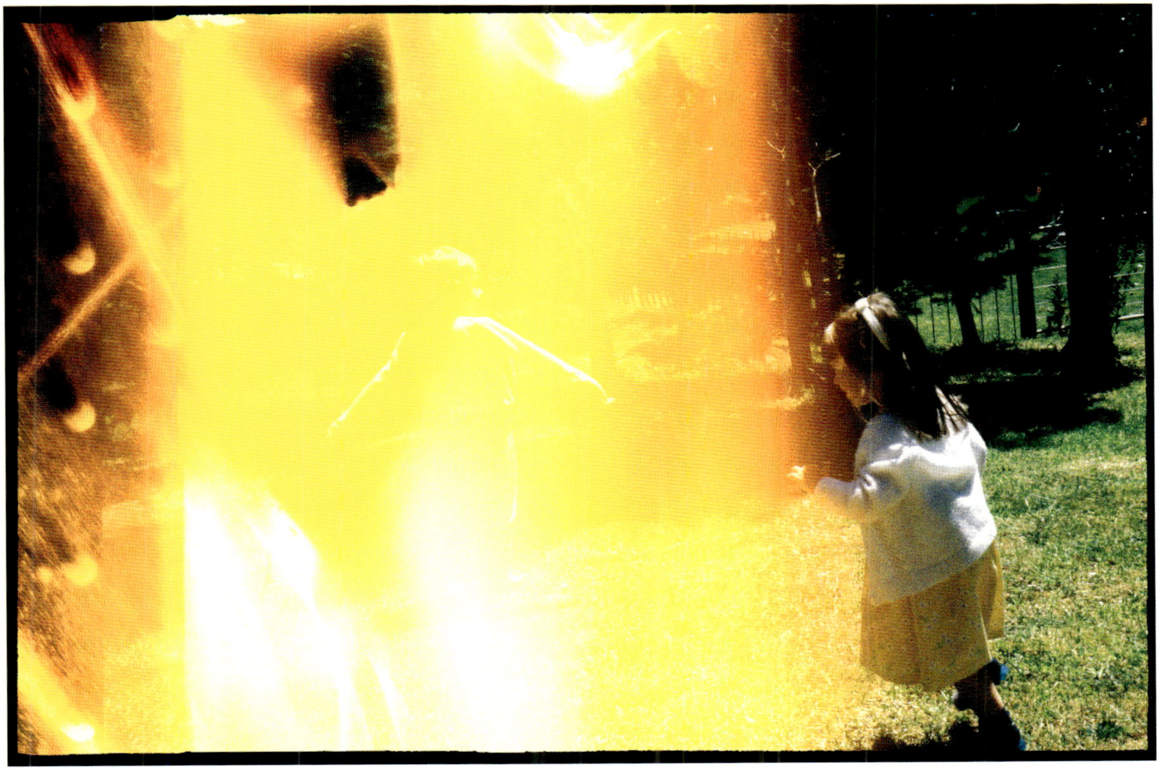

Follow, 2000

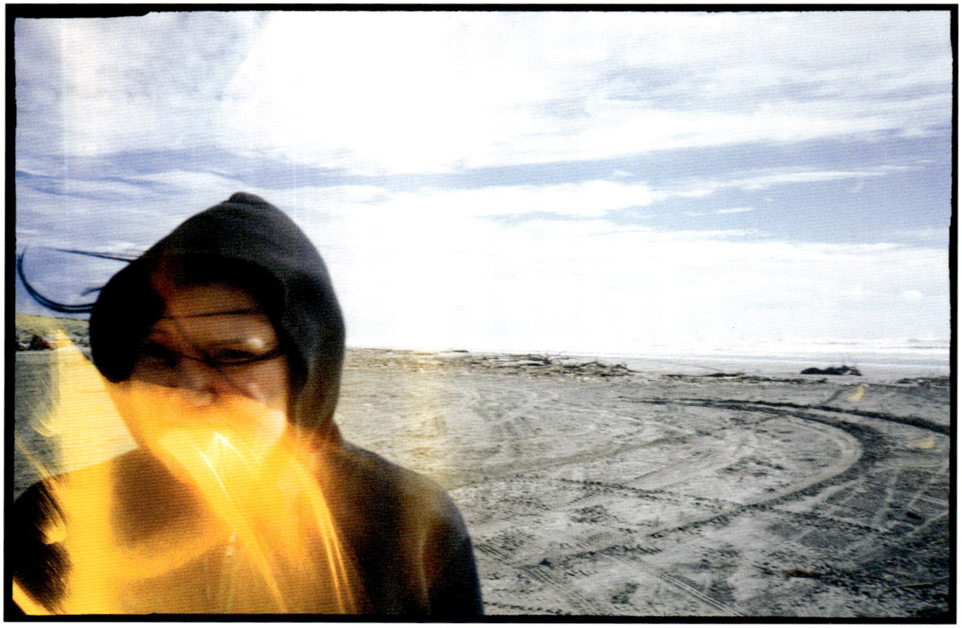

Kapiti New Year, 2000

Edit

No ringside seats compensate
nothing new to be said
about a job completed
for you by others
in windowless rooms.

A half-soul in transit
the man you were
for one short season
has been pruned
removed
to a well-groomed graveyard
that smells like popcorn.

(1992)

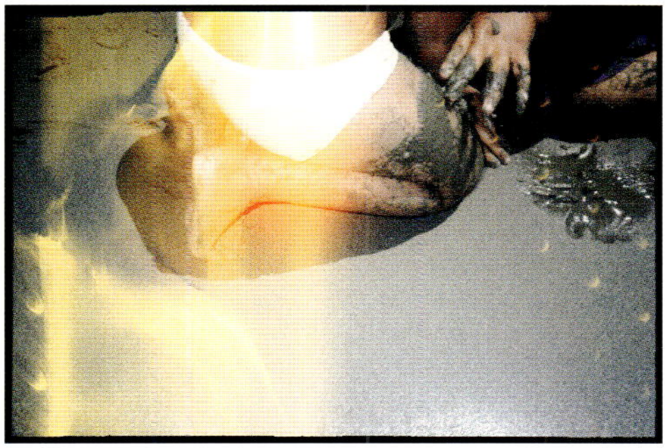

Lyall Bay, 2000

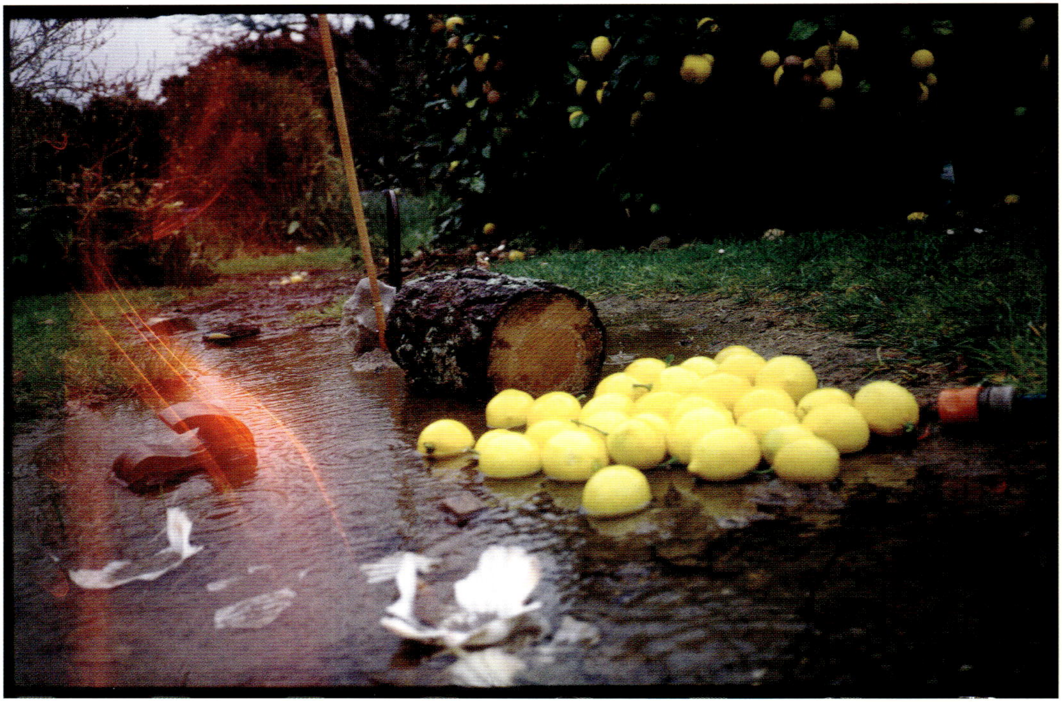

Fun House Lemons, 2000

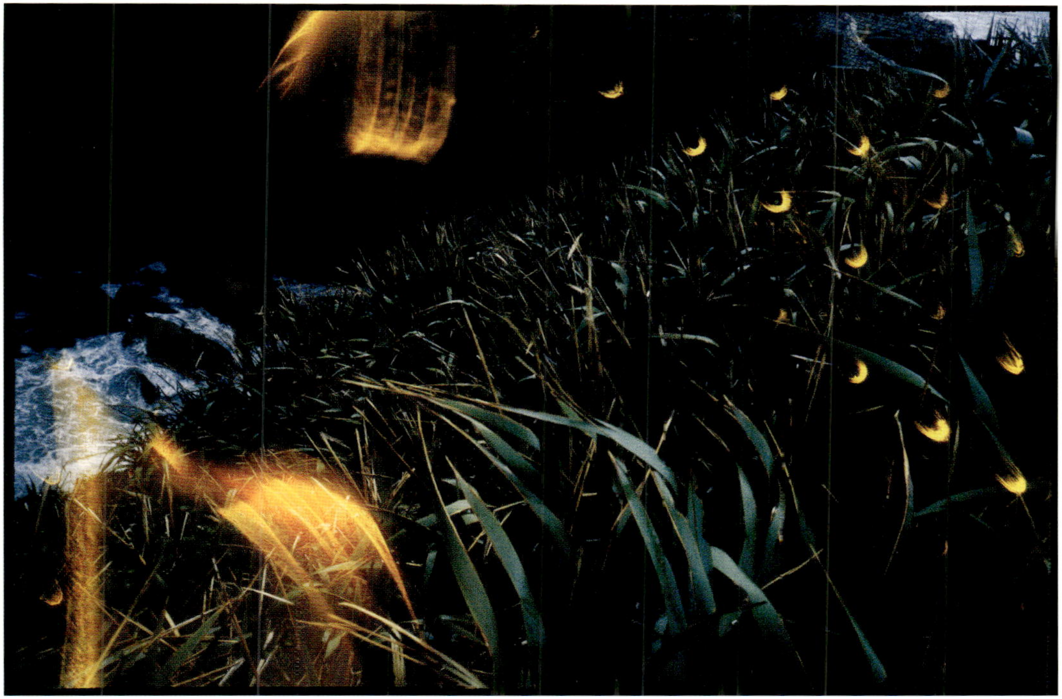

Pancakes, 2000

Lead

Moths are being burnt tonight, halfway into the late shift, by men propped up with cigarettes. Smoke ribbons unfurl in the harsh fluorescent light and disappear in a twinkling blizzard of metal and choking bugs that hides the ceiling. The younger men calculate how much more money they'll make for not sleeping this week. The older men roll the cigarettes. One man consoles the other by staying awake, covering for him when he naps on the toilet, away from the foreman's blue eye. There are coffee pot holes, and the gravelly work floor sparkles with scratchy rag-lung spit spots pumped out by black-blooded heart muscle. At dawn they let the showers run until the water is good and warm, so as not to startle themselves when they step in to wash the dust from their grey hair and skin.

(1979)

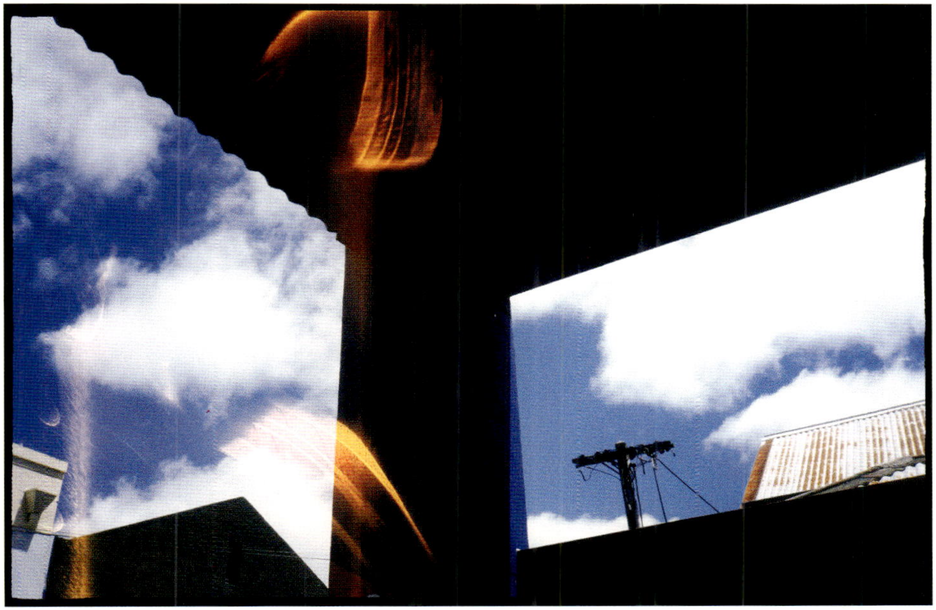

Spring, Wellington, 2000

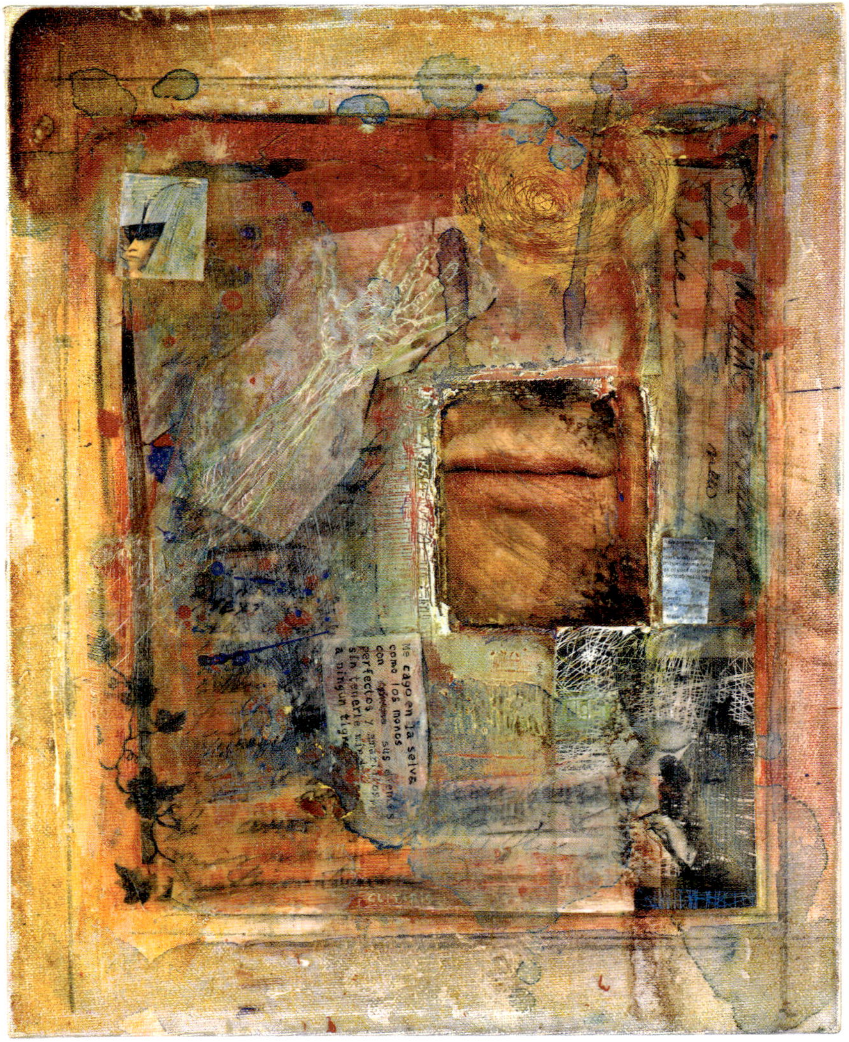

Self-Portrait, April, 1999–2002

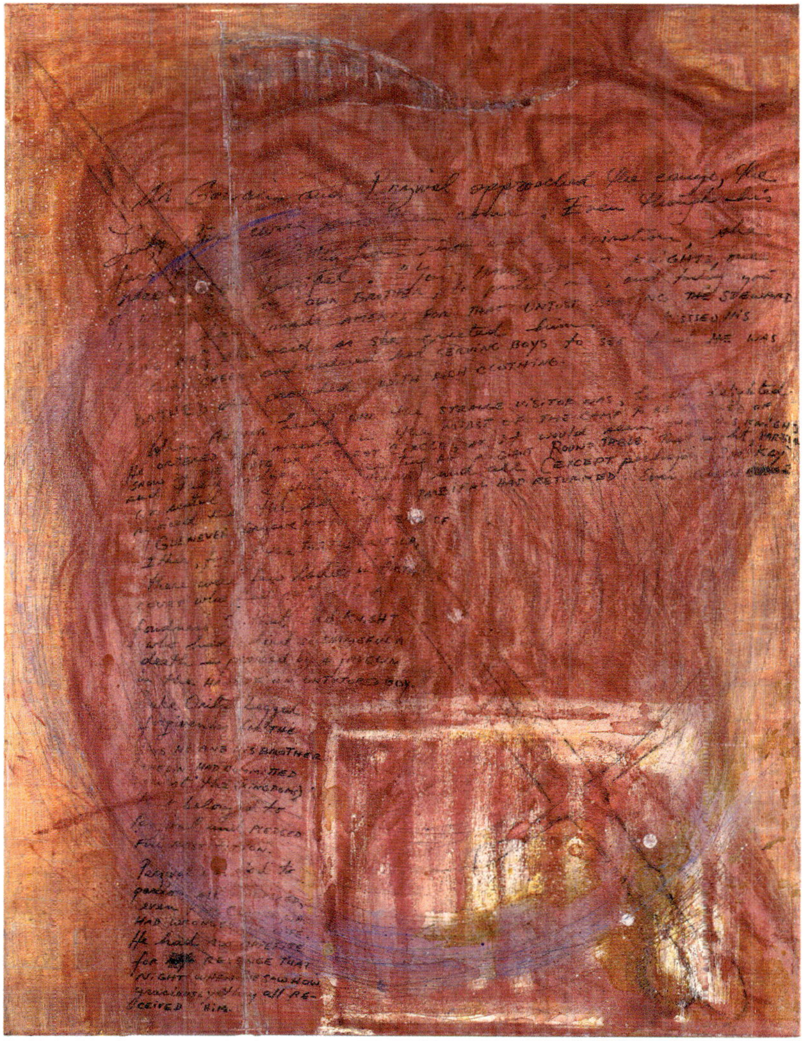

Parzival's Back, 1999–2002

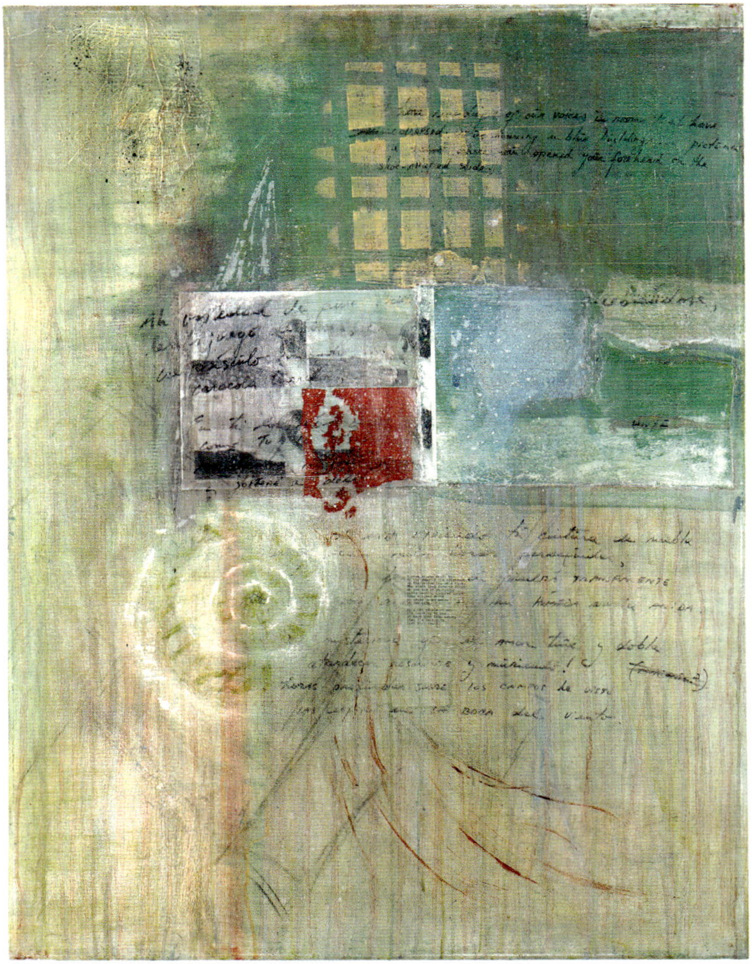

Gulf Stream, 1999–2002

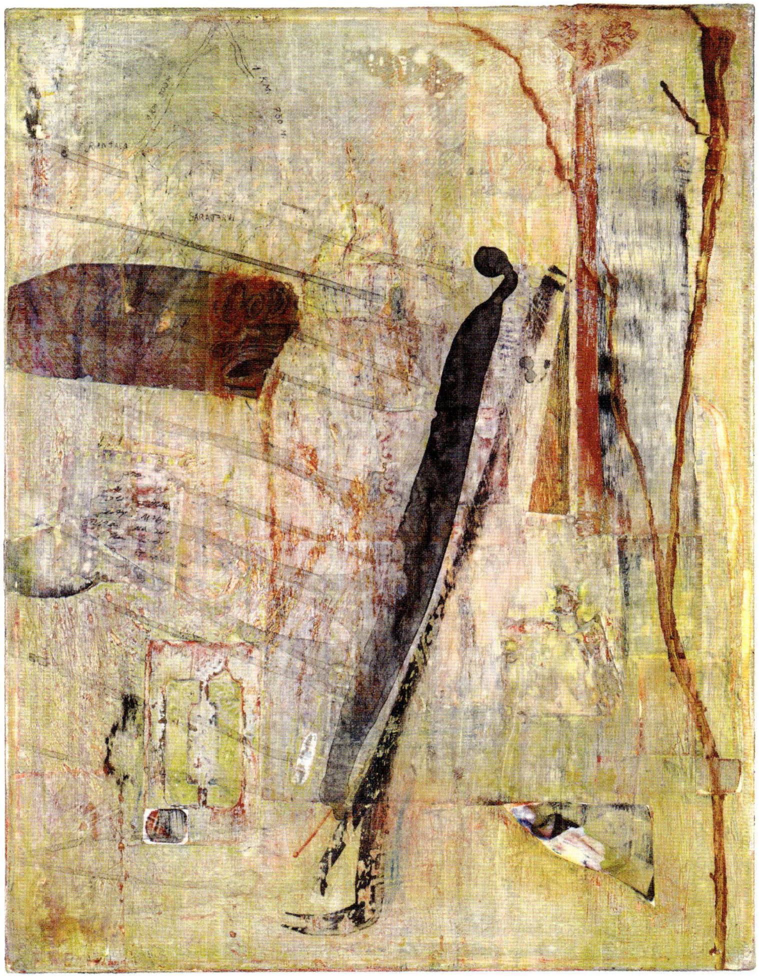

Finland Aerial, Harvest, 2000–02

Hallowe'en

They were always giving birth, always pregnant, always taking fucking for granted. They were not being brave when they dug up the skulls of their past lovers in the middle of the night and painted them for use as Jack O'Lanterns. It was summer and they were crazy about each other. In the past week the weather has turned bad and they've stuffed a sheet into the stovepipe to keep out the wind. It is torn and bloodstained from the time he convalesced on it after tearing up his ankle in a motorcycle accident. It smells of that time, of arnica and sweat. They need more than a sheet to remember what bound them. They need wood for the stove. Lately, they've been fighting over those heads, wanting to know whose was whose. She's been splitting them with the kindling axe when the kids have fallen asleep and he is taking his evening bath. Up to his ears in oily bubbles, he hears the bone splintering, as well as the occasional bad swing that takes a divot out of the rotten floorboards of the back porch, and thinks it's probably good exercise. He remembers standing holding hands with her outside their locked car, keys visible in moonlight on the front seat: freezing on the prairie, laughing at themselves.

(1990)

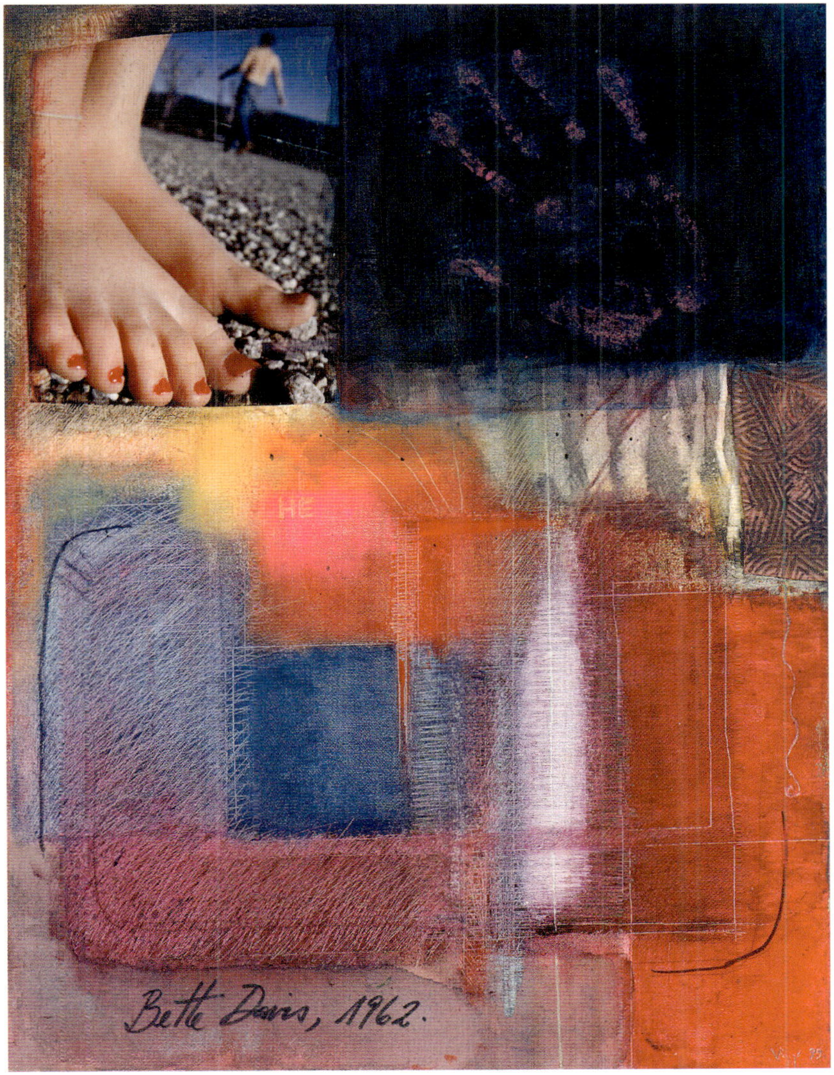

Bette Davis, 1962, 1999

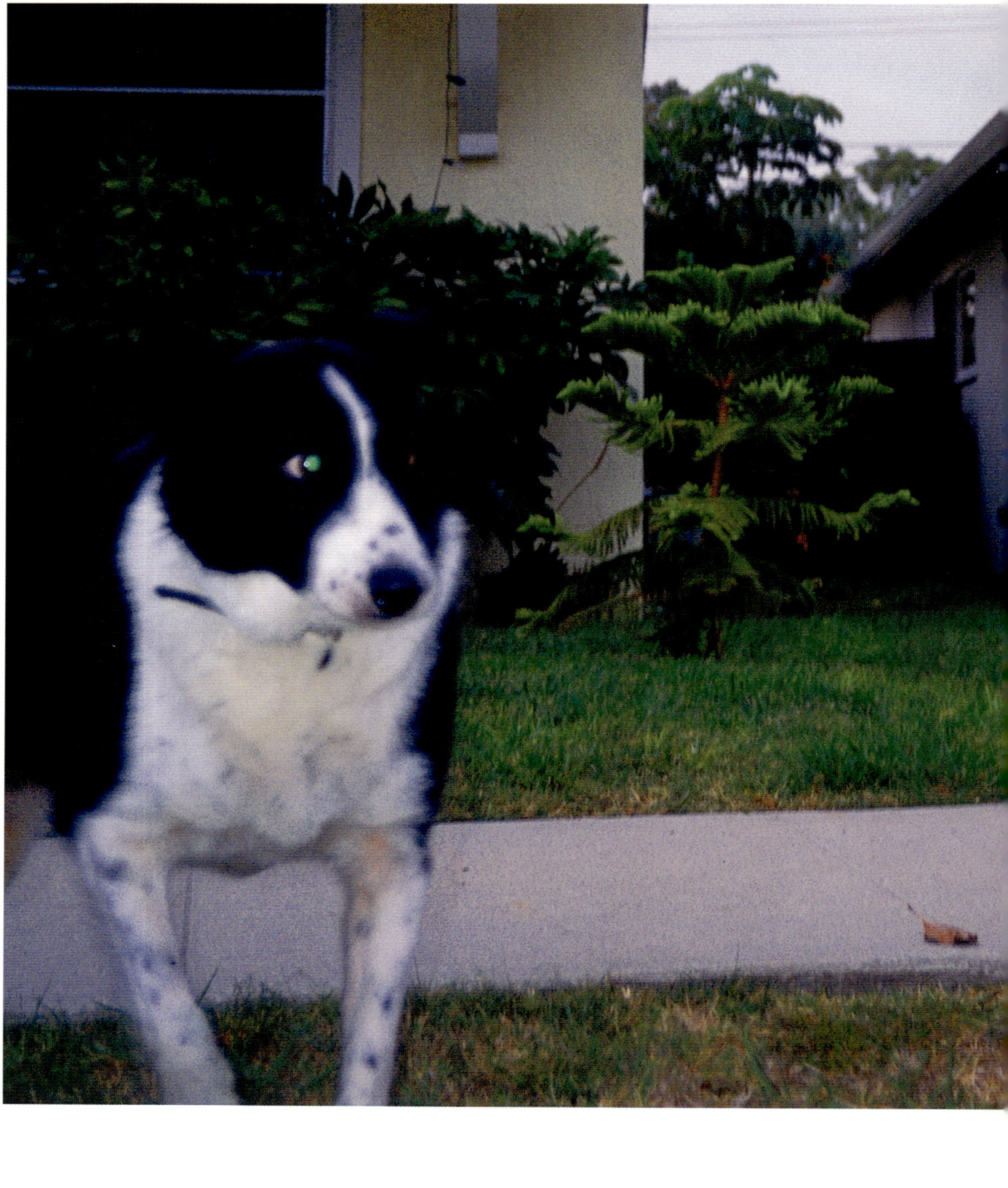

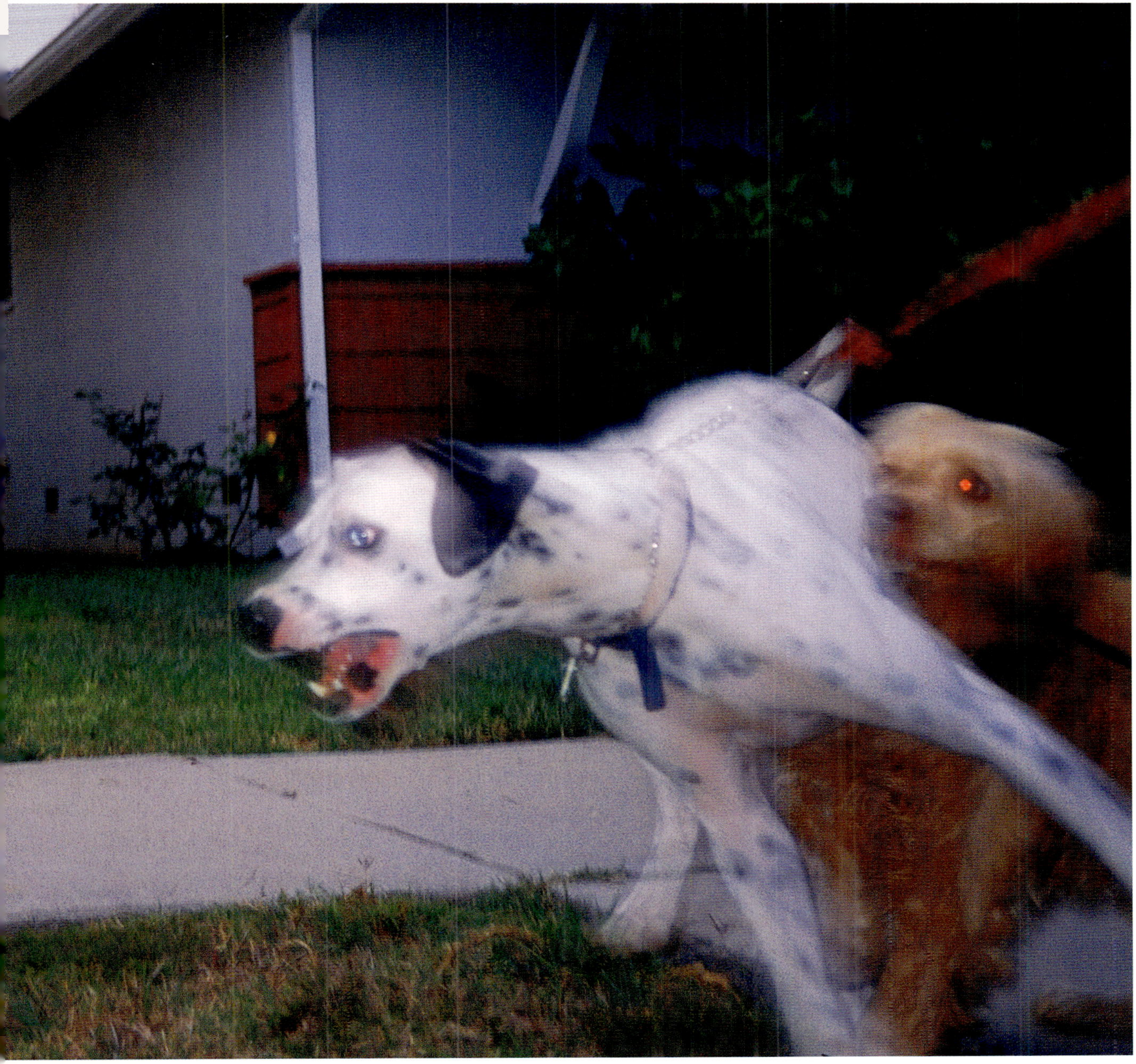

Scared Brigit, 1998

Communion

1.
We've left shore somehow
become the friends
of early theory
close enough to speak
desire and pain of absence
of mistakes we'd make
given the chance.

Each smile returned
makes harder avoiding
dreams that see us
lying in early evening
curtain shadows, skin
safe against skin.
Bloom of compassion
respect for moments
eyes lock turns
forever into one more
veil that falls away.

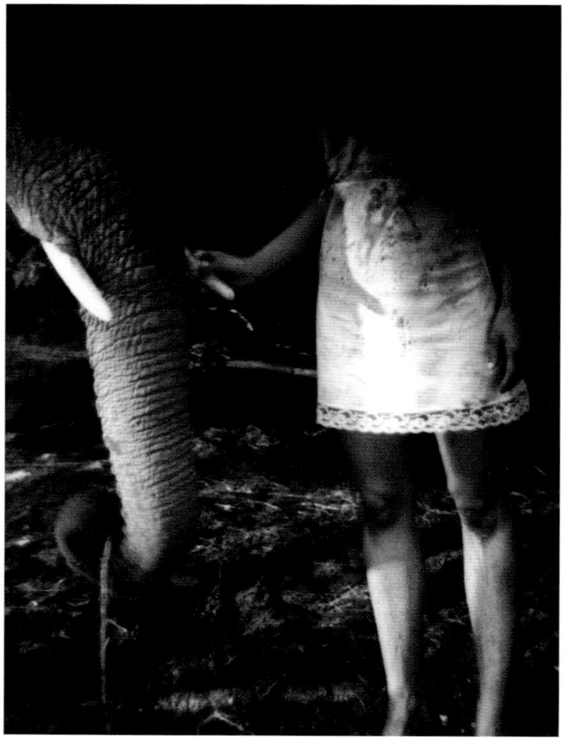

Daisy, 1994

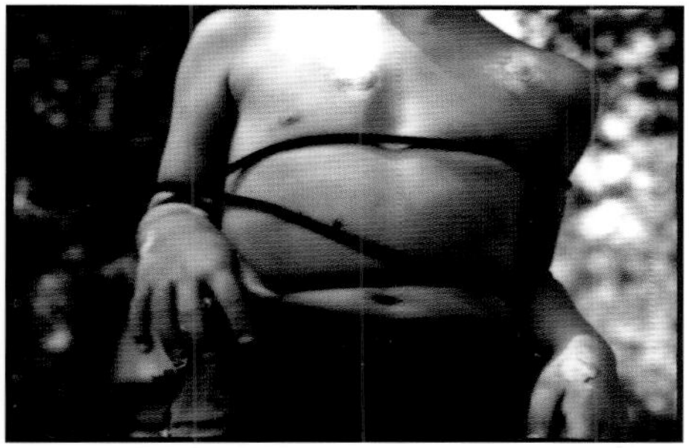

Lesson, 1997

2.
This after seeing you
last night, first time
smelling you with
permission: shoulders to
wonder openly at
as carefully kissed
as those arms
waited impossibly on.
They've held me now
and your breath
down my back
sent away night air
that had me shaking
in the unlit Anglican
doorway.

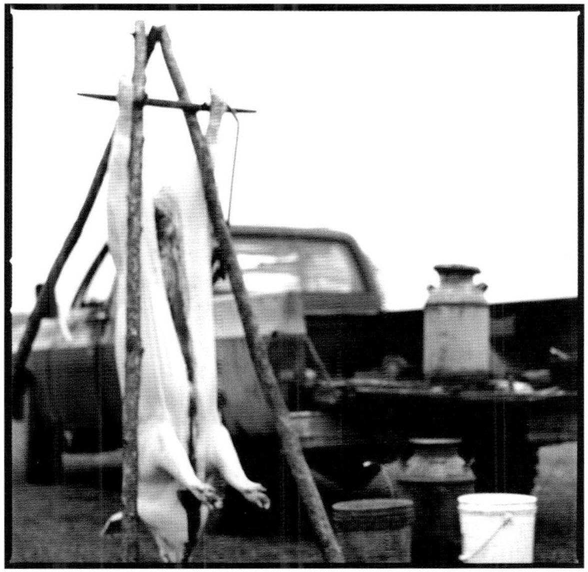

Slaughter Sequence, #4, 1985

3.

Are we ruined for
finding our faces fit
and want to know more
about morning? Is
friendship cancelled
if we can't call
each other anymore
in amnesia, invite
ourselves to last glances
under suspicious clocks
telling us when we've
had enough?

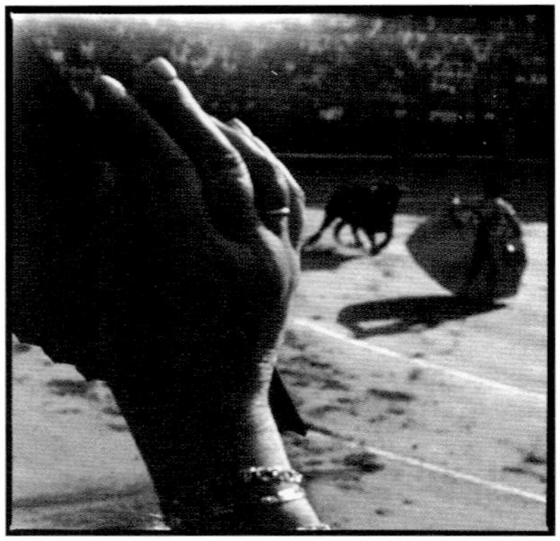

Madrid, 1995

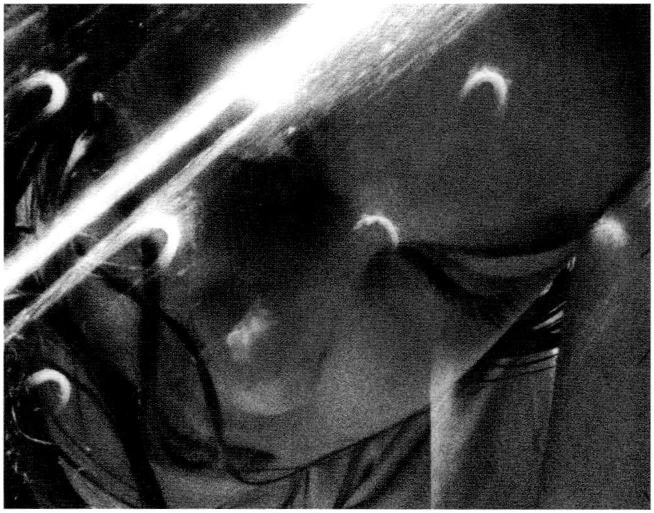

Medium, 2000

4.

Your steady hands
cradling my grateful
skull: were you taking
in my face to
save an image
you've rarely allowed
yourself after leaving
that cold alcove?
Am I a photograph
you gaze at in
moments of weakness?

You ordered me
off my knees
into your arms.
Wasn't to beg
that I knelt; only
to see you once
from below.

Tried to say something
that filled my mouth
and longed to rest
in your ear.
Don't dare write
it down for fear it'll
become words, just
words.

(1999–2002)

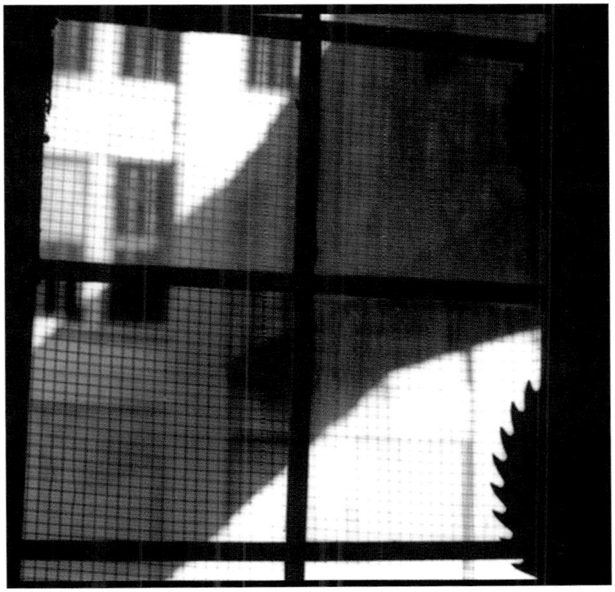

Greenpoint, 1997

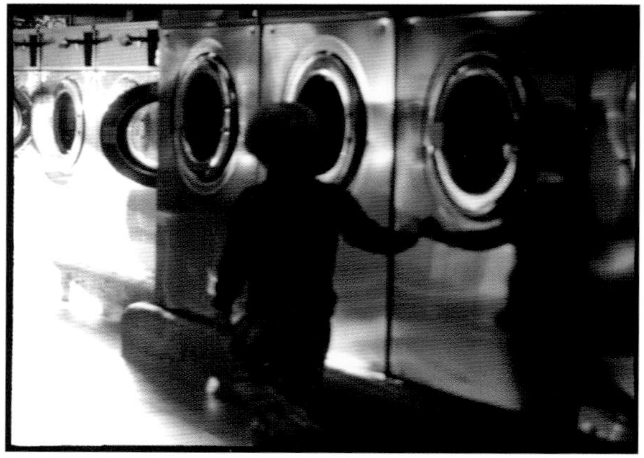

Sunday, NYC, 1985

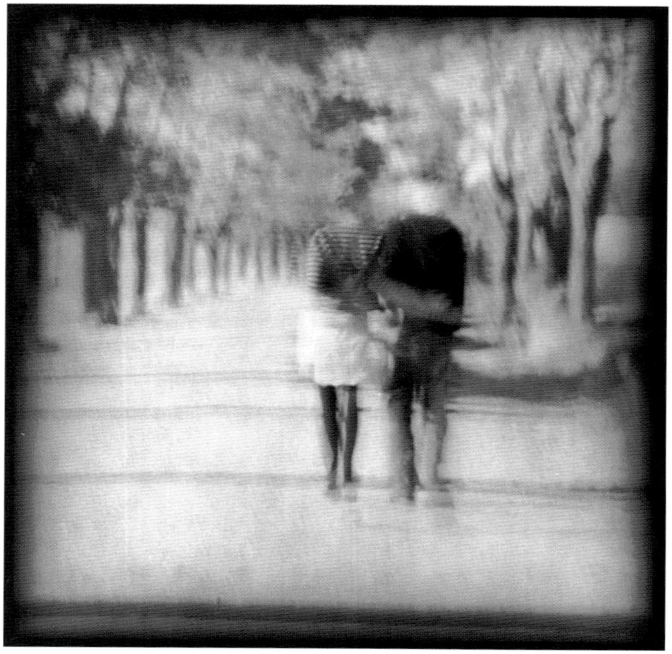

Christina y Ray, 1995

You are sweating in your sleep
on our rented bed
like a lost summer cloud
pierced by a jet heard
only when it's gone.

The birds above the waterfall
drink mist from giant leaves
then fly over the edge.

(1992)

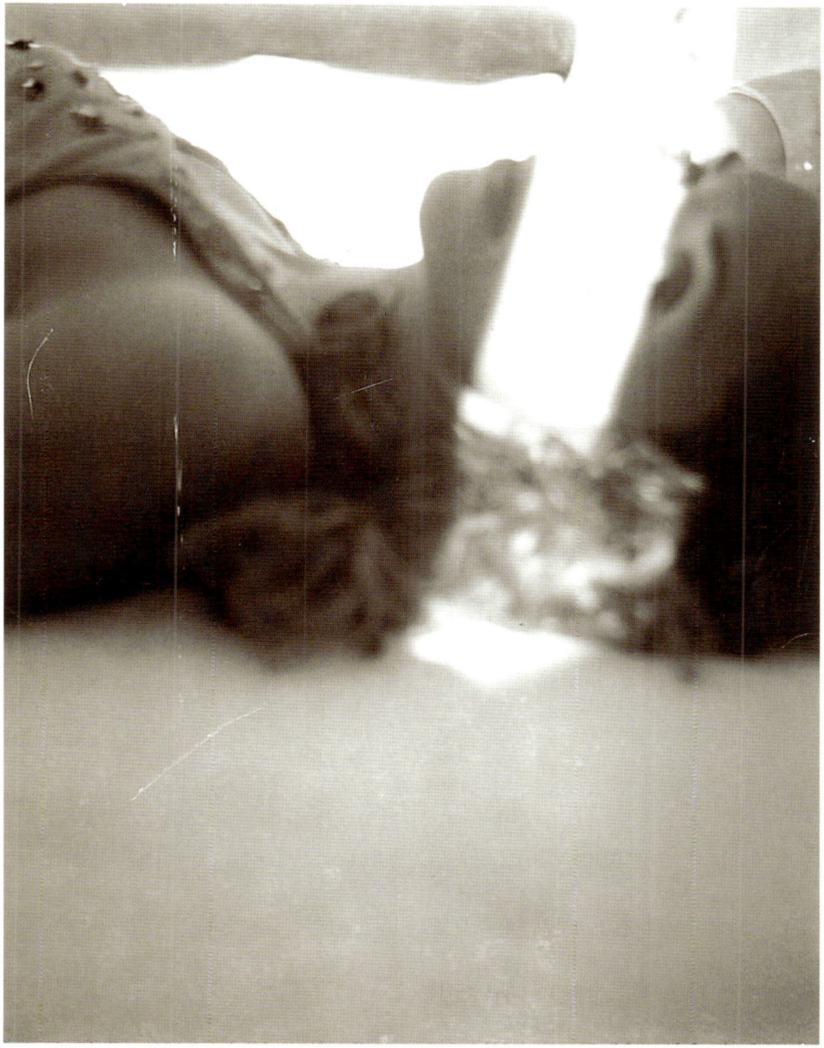

Laura, 1993

Sueño del Retiro, 2001

Castro's

Am I as gone as October
at this table, two
from the one we talked
at for hours of plans
for summer and rivers,
where I marvelled at
the new mystery just
inches of white linen
away?

You are still present,
dressed warmer than
necessary, tame enough
to be understood, to
say that you too are
curious about how
we might go places.
The waiter looms,
inadvertently breaking
the news that you're
really back home, perhaps
in a relieved apron state
that may fit you just fine,
for all I ever knew.

(2000–02)

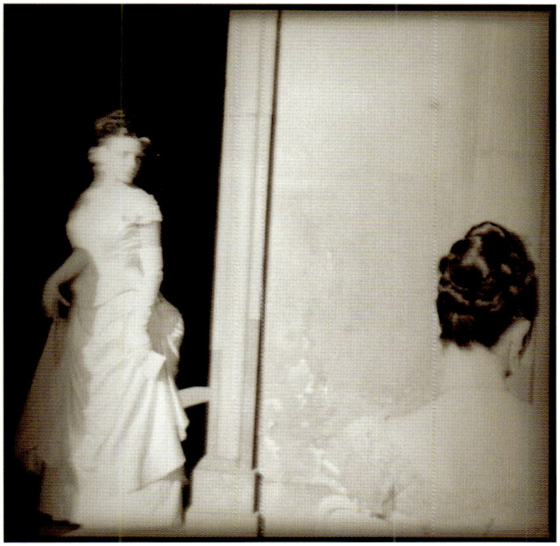

Florence. 1995

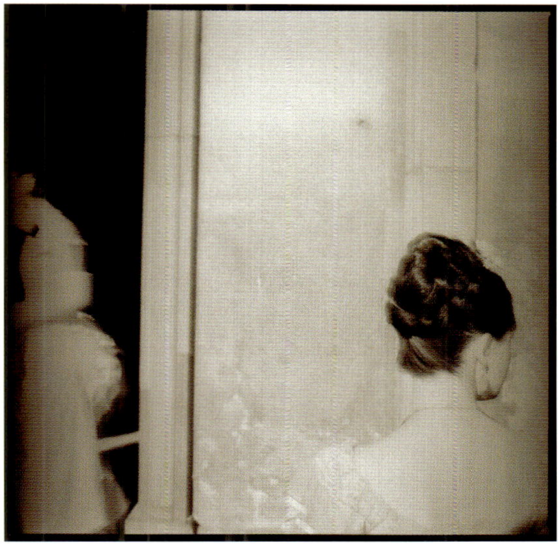

Florence #2, 1995

Last Leg

After driving the first forty miles of the day
you accused me of ignoring you.
Now I am waiting for the next volley
but it isn't coming.
I've been thinking for an hour since
and I don't know what you meant.
All you probably wanted was to trade a few words.
I didn't.
My mind has been on road things.
I see that the ocotillo is greening
the sage looks like new.
Crows everywhere.
Some of the washes are wet
and there's a three-day grass mantle
on the highway shoulder.
Even the cottonwoods show signs
of waking up.
But now that you have accused me
I don't feel like mentioning these things.
Or the roadkills.
Or the Colorado
which we just crossed
as you bore down on yet another postcard.
Maybe you're right
maybe this silence is oppressive
indicating some great underlying disorder.
But the year has already begun
and this car is running perfect.

(1990)

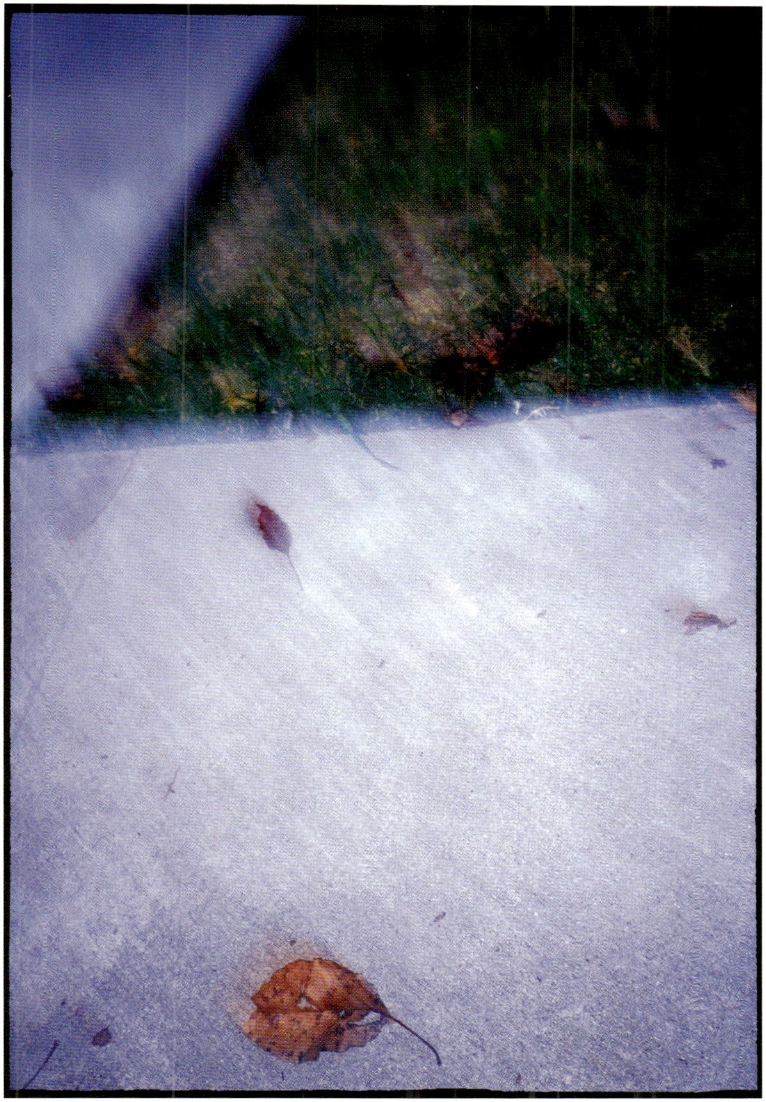

Santa Ana, 1998

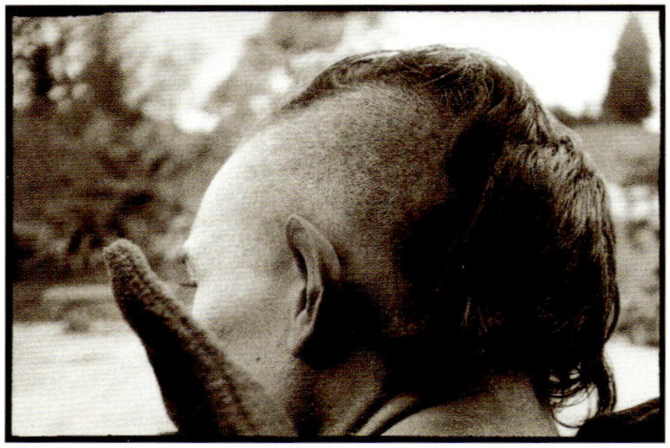

Elf Head, 1999

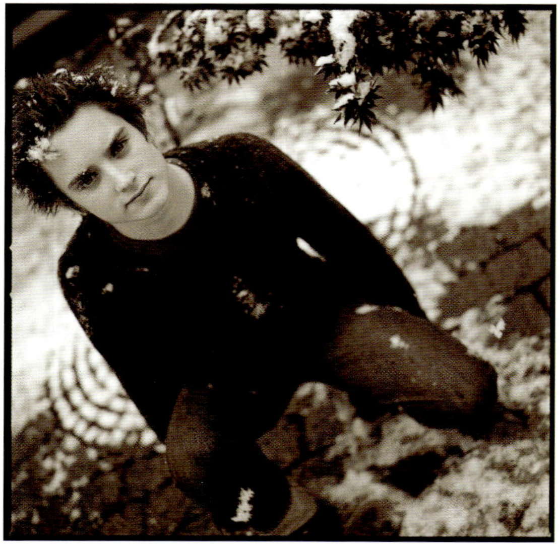

Te Anau, 1999

They roll over on the swells
and forget themselves
floating on a sea littered
with broken oars and scraps
of sails. They'll hang on chains
around teenage necks, long after
sinking, piece by piece, away from
the moon.

(1990)

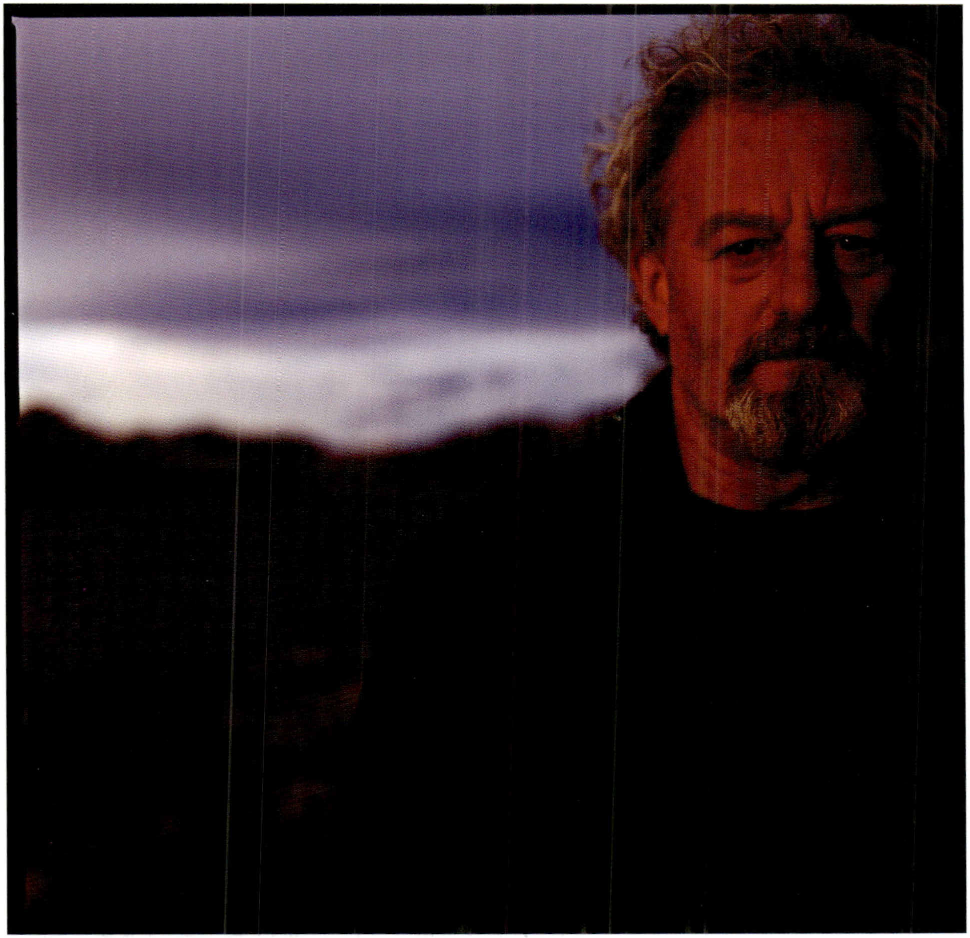

Rohan, 2000

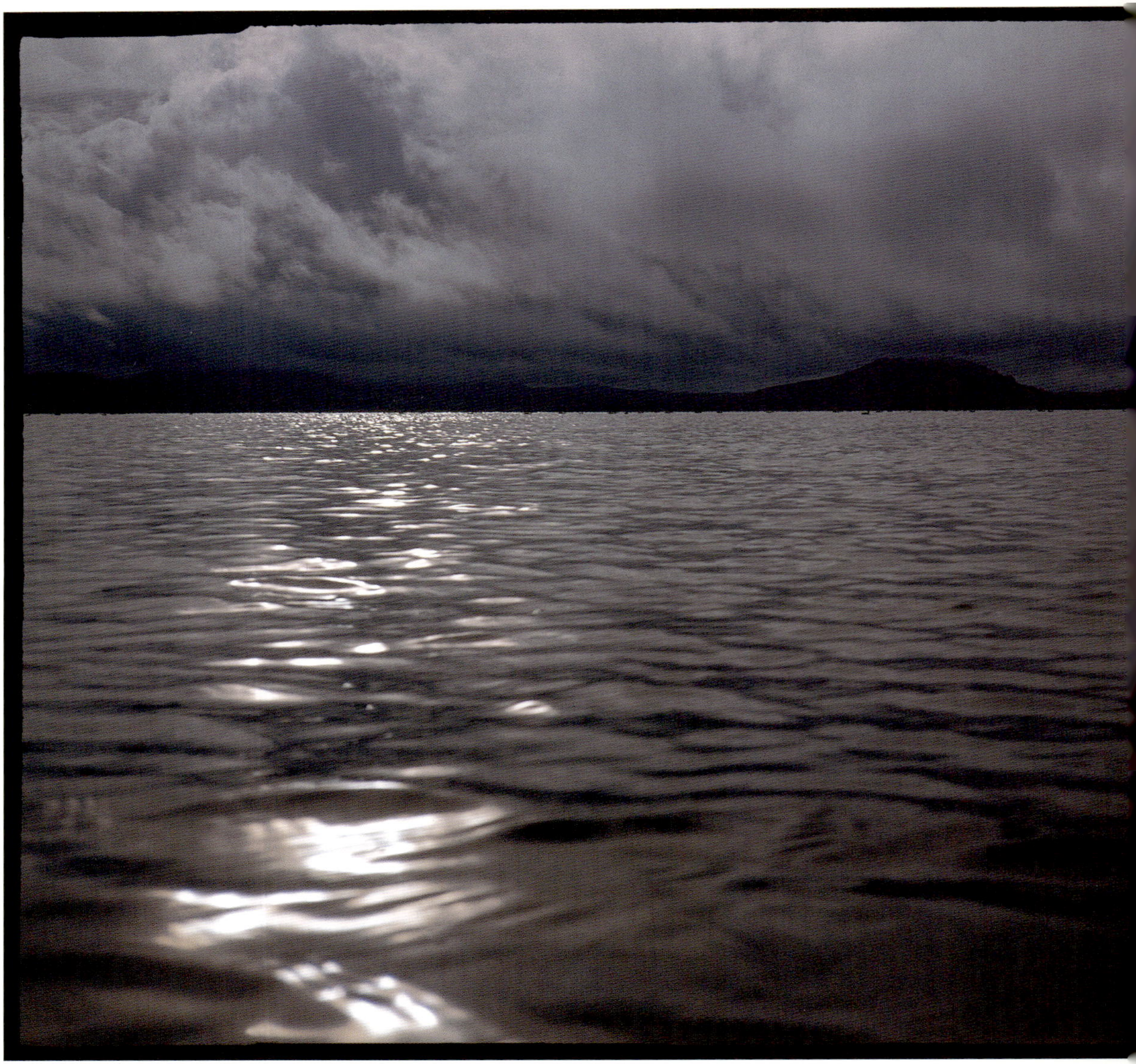

Taupo, 2000

Oceans take our secrets
what we don't want to see or smell anymore.
We feel anonymous
we feel clean
when we throw our past away.
It will wash, we think.
It will sink
it will drift far from this shore.
It will disappear.
Maybe the fish will eat our words
maybe lost or spurned loves
will help deep-sea feathery green plants grow.

Now and again
I find myself walking on the wet, hard-packed sand
looking for tears and exotic messages
in the creeping, reaching water
that just misses touching my toes.
Sometimes there's something clear and obvious
like a fingernail or a plastic bag
though I'll never know for sure
who threw them away.
Once I found a wedding ring
uncovered by the receding tide.
I didn't touch it.
I was already married.

(1991)

First Light

1.
Even now, out of
radio range and time,
you advance, insistent,
aglow. Wet forelock
exactly where it fell
across your reddened brow,
eyes lit and daring
all comers. Mostly,
though, I remember
you keeping a
mingling distance
as the company grew
and began to sway
around three or
four in the afternoon.

My hands have healed
and still reach through
moonless dawn for
your nape, clavicle, crow's
feet, eyelids as I drive
into your green country.
Reminders appear like
lines of frost as sun
reaches steering wheel
and raspy coffee consonants
start piercing static.
Torn knuckles sealed,
making less of wounds
I'll not forget as easily
as you forgot to write.
You pushed my arms
out from our hips, bloody
paws suspended, flopping
to make the only breeze in
the valley. Can what's now
freely given be acceptable,
the uncluttered embrace
of another welcomed as
your echo unravels?

I've traversed clotheslines
sagging in dewlight to see
your candles, to kneel on
pavement and hold out
notes left trapped
on my windshield,
folded over twice for
privacy, eagerly and often
re-read. The possible scent
of your careless hand
scribbling, of thumb
dragging, easily opening
my mouth for anything
you wish me to swallow.

2.
And you, little god: do
you avoid burning finger
tips when shielding moths
from your bedside light?
Can you keep your father's
heart safe under your
pillow? Will you soon
wonder why I didn't warn
you well enough how
it would hurt to lose
your petals and grow
scars on your hands?

(1999—2002)

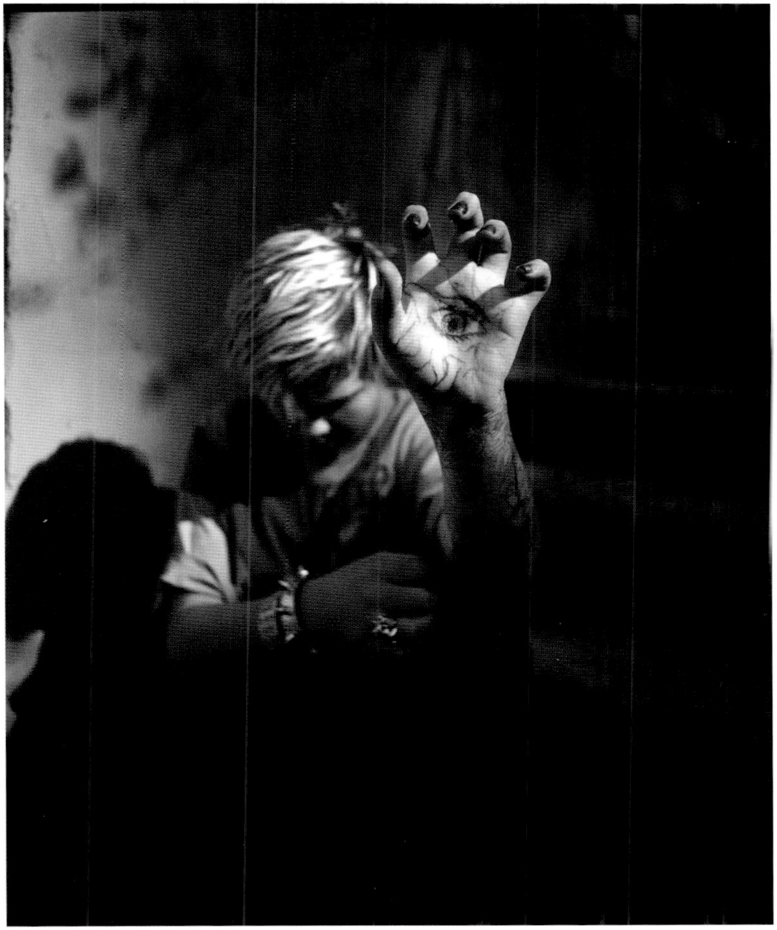

Topanga, 2002

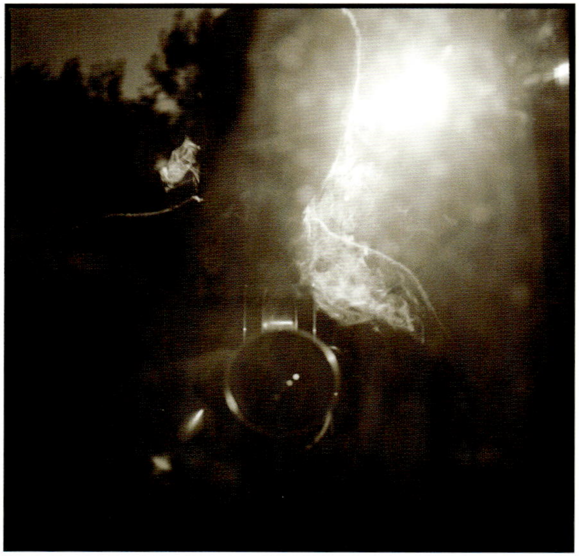

Self-Portrait, Winter, 2002

Seek not the favour
of the multitude;
it is seldom got by
honest and lawful means.
But seek the testimony
of the few; and number
not the voices, but
weigh them.

—Immanuel Kant

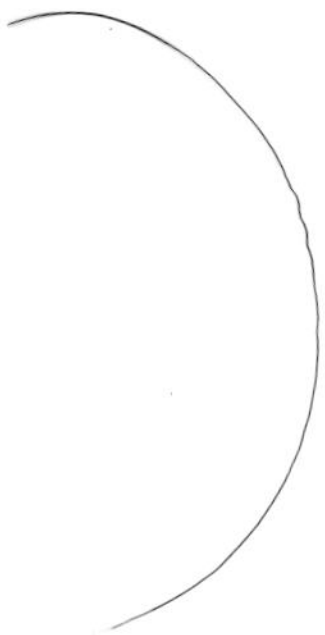